The Survival Guide

for Newly Qualified Social Workers in Adult and Mental Health Services

of related interest

The Survival Guide for Newly Qualified Child and Family Social Workers
Hitting the Ground Running
Helen Donnellan and Gordon Jack
ISBN 978 1 84310 989 1

Handbook for Practice Learning in Social Work and Social Care
Knowledge and Theory
2nd edition
Edited by Joyce Lishman
ISBN 978 1 84310 186 4

Reflective Practice in Mental Health
Advanced Psychosocial Practice with Children, Adolescents and Adults
Edited by Martin Webber and Jack Nathan
ISBN 978 1 84905 029 6
Reflective Practice in Social Care series

Good Practice in Safeguarding Adults
Working Effectively in Adult Protection
Edited by Jacki Pritchard
ISBN 978 1 84310 699 9
Good Practice in Health, Social Care and Criminal Justice series

The Post-Qualifying Handbook for Social Workers
Edited by Wade Tovey
ISBN 978 1 84310 428 5

Competence in Social Work Practice
A Practical Guide for Students and Professionals
2nd edition
Edited by Kieran O'Hagan
ISBN 978 1 84310 485 8

Social Work Under Pressure
How to Overcome Stress, Fatigue and Burnout in the Workplace
Kate van Heugten
ISBN 978 1 84905 116 3

Recording Skills in Safeguarding Adults
Best Practice and Evidential Requirements
Jacki Pritchard
with Simon Leslie
ISBN 978 1 84905 112 5

The Survival Guide

for Newly Qualified Social Workers in Adult and Mental Health Services

Hitting the Ground Running

Diane Galpin, Jenny Bigmore and Jo Parker

Jessica Kingsley *Publishers*
London and Philadelphia

Crown copyright material is reproduced with the permission of the
controller of the HMSO and the Queen's Printer for Scotland.

First published in 2012
by Jessica Kingsley Publishers
116 Pentonville Road
London N1 9JB, UK
and
400 Market Street, Suite 400
Philadelphia, PA 19106, USA

www.jkp.com

Library of Congress Cataloging in Publication Data
Galpin, Diane.
The survival guide for newly qualified social workers in adult and mental
health services : hitting the ground running / Diane Galpin, Jenny Bigmore and
Jo Parker.
  p. cm.
Includes bibliographical references and index.
ISBN 978-1-84905-158-3 (alk. paper)
 1. Social workers--Great Britain--Handbooks, manuals, etc. I. Bigmore,
Jenny, 1956- II. Parker, Jo, 1975- III. Title.
HV245.G345 2012
362.2'04250941--dc23
                    2011025156

British Library Cataloguing in Publication Data
A CIP catalogue record for this book is available from the British Library

ISBN 978 1 84905 158 3
eISBN 978 0 85700 557 1

Printed and bound in Great Britain

Contents

Conclusion

Figures

Tables

Boxes

Introduction

The purpose of this book

The first year in practice is a critical time in a social worker's professional development, and the value of a formal programme of support has been identified as central to enabling graduates make the move from student to professional. This has led to the development of the Newly Qualified Social Worker (NQSW) frameworks for newly qualified social workers employed in adult and mental health services across the four countries that make up the UK. Their purpose is to provide clarity in understanding the respective roles and responsibilities of both employee and employer in developing a workforce that delivers high-quality social work. Government and society expect social workers to take an active role in developing and demonstrating a high level of skill, knowledge and professionalism when working with those whom they may encounter.

This book is intended to support you in meeting those expectations. Each chapter aims to help you negotiate the journey into professional practice as effectively, and painlessly, as possible, drawing on the experiences of those who have already embarked on this journey and the authors' experience of supporting newly qualified social workers in their personal and professional development in post-qualifying education. Each chapter explores common themes identified as important, providing theoretical and practical support.

The content of this book is not intended as a blueprint for social work in adult and mental health services, nor to specify what practice should be like, but rather to enable readers to identify ways in which they can make the transition from student to professional and expand their thinking, skills and knowledge beyond the point of initial qualification – in essence, to bring together academic learning and practice experience to facilitate professional development in your first year, and beyond.

Who is this book for?

Whilst the primary focus in this book is on individuals coming to the end of their qualifying programmes and new entrants to the profession, of equal importance is the full engagement of your new employer in supporting the delivery of high-quality social work services. Managers, supervisors, training and developmental personnel have a central role and responsibility in supporting all NQSWs to meet any statutory or regulatory requirements. This book can provide a useful *aide mémoire* for them in understanding your journey from student to professional, as well as undertaking their own particular roles effectively.

Key areas, and issues commonly identified as important for those embarking on a new professional role, are discussed, and information provided is transferable across adult service user groups and practice settings. However, each reader will be on their own developmental journey and what works for one might not for another; therefore, please take an open and critical approach to understanding and applying the contents of this book.

How this book is organised

The book is divided into three parts:

- Part I: Finding Your Feet (Chapters 1–3)

- Part II: Finding Your Way (Chapters 4 and 5)

- Part III: Finding the Way Forward (Chapters 6–8)

The individual chapters in each part aim to provide support and guidance as you embark on your professional career.

Each chapter provides analysis and guidance on a specific area of development identified as relevant to professional social work practice and provides research, theoretical perspectives and activities that can be used at an individual level to support an NQSW. The aim of the activities is to help individuals to stop, think, reflect and plan. This provides one way in which to consolidate the skills and knowledge developed in formal education and training, and transfer them into practice. Throughout the book practice scenarios and the reflections of NQSWs already embarking on this journey are used to identify common themes and issues, suggesting that you may well not be alone in any feelings you are experiencing, which may be reassuring!

Contents of the book

Chapter 1 focuses on the transition from student to professional. This is a period characterised by change, and whilst this will be something you have been working towards for a number of years, it can still prove daunting. However, the good news is that by managing this period you can begin to make a real difference to those you come into contact with, right from the start of your career. You will be bringing a fresh pair of eyes to the organisation and can challenge the status quo. However, you need to be aware of where you are in relation to your skills, knowledge and experience and to understand how best to communicate your views in an established team. The importance of this is apparent in a serious case review discussed in Chapter 1, which highlights how confidence, combined with the ability to openly, and respectfully, question existing practice, might contribute to professional practice.

As you make the transition from student to professional the first stop on your journey will be 'NQSW'. NQSW will help redefine who you are in the first year of practice. Chapter 2 provides a basic understanding of NQSW status and what it might mean for you. The UK is divided into four countries and each has its own NQSW framework, which will help shape your first year in practice. Whilst all are slightly different, they share the common theme of a partnership approach to ensuring that you develop the necessary skills and knowledge to practise both competently and confidently as a social worker. As an NQSW you will be expected to take a proactive approach in endeavouring to develop, deliver and maintain a high standard of social work practice. Chapter 2 identifies the framework relevant to you and provides guidance on how best to make it work for you.

Even though the NQSW framework is there to ease the transition from student to professional, starting work in a new job is always nerve-racking, but never more so than when you are entering a profession as important as social work where you will work with people who may be at risk, or vulnerable. Chapter 3 guides you through the process of starting work in a new organisation, offering practical advice on any preparation you might undertake and providing valuable information regarding the process and purpose of induction and what it means for you. This chapter also helps you to plan how to make those all-important first connections with your peers and other professional groups so as to facilitate a positive relationship within, and across, organisational contexts in order to develop the meaningful partnership working that makes a real difference to those who use adult and mental health services.

As you develop purposeful and professional relationships, you will also need to ensure that you have a strong sense of your own professional identity. Whilst a variety of professions may undertake similar tasks within adult and mental health services, each has its own distinctive identity and voice. Chapter 4 highlights the importance of developing and maintaining your professional identity as a social worker to ensure that, when working with adults, what you do is informed by practice that views the individual from a variety of sometimes conflicting theoretical perspectives, and by professional values that influence decision making and outcomes for service users.

Of course, much of your practice will be shaped by policy and legislation, which ultimately determines what roles and tasks you will be expected to engage in. These will change over time as government, society and professional bodies determine the purpose of social work and the agencies with whom you will work. Ensuring that you keep up to date with the evolution of professional roles and tasks will require commitment and sustained motivation on your part. Social work, for many, is more than 'a job'. Individuals are frequently attracted to the profession because they feel it is a 'meaningful' occupation. Professionals can also experience stress and burnout as they become bogged down by what seem like never-ending bureaucracy and change; however, there are ways in which you can develop and sustain your motivation, even in the midst of change. Chapter 5 provides advice and guidance for understanding the relationship between policy, legislation and the potential professional roles and tasks you will be expected to engage in, as well as for keeping motivated to ensure that you keep the meaningful aspects of practice in focus. This chapter aims to provide a foundation from which to develop your understanding of what you do in practice, and, which is just as important, why.

Maintaining motivation and meaning will require more than your best efforts, and the organisation you work for will also have a role in supporting you in the day-to-day business of complex practice. The one central, and constant, companion of good social work practice is supervision. Whilst research and regulatory frameworks, without exception, attest to the importance of good supervision in supporting good social work practice, it is still sometimes undervalued and overlooked, especially once you are engaged in the cut-and-thrust of practice, where complex cases, risky situations and organisational needs can marginalise supervisory arrangements and participation. Chapter 6 clearly outlines the rationale for supervision, identifying the different forms you might engage in, and provides guidance on participating in this important activity. This chapter cannot guarantee that you will receive the best supervision, but it can ensure that you know how to do your best to maximise the supervisory experience.

The preceding chapters will have provided the foundations from which to develop a strategy that works to help you maximise your potential in the first year of practice. Even though you may follow every suggestion, complete every exercise, engage in every activity, you will still experience times when you feel 'stressed'. Stress is not necessarily a negative emotion; we all need a certain amount of stress in our lives, as this acts as a motivator. However, there is a fine line between stress that energises and stress that leaves you feeling unable to contend with difficulties. Chapter 7 provides crucial advice and guidance on how to manage stress. It is important to be aware of its existence and how it manifests itself, if you are not to fall foul of it. One way in which you can manage stress is to ensure that you have adequate support networks around you, and this chapter provides guidance on developing such networks. Whilst stress might be an area you would prefer to ignore at present, if you want a career at the vanguard of a profession such as social work, it's something you ignore at your peril.

Having completed your formal education and training, and traversed the chasm between the rhetoric and reality of contemporary social work in the course of your first year in practice, you should take time to stop and reflect on the journey so far, and think ahead to the future. Where do you want to be in five years' time, and how will you get there? What role will continuing professional development (CPD) have to play? Chapter 8 focuses on how to stop, look back, and use reflection to help you move forward, providing guidance on possible CPD routes that you might consider as you plan for your future.

The Conclusion provides a brief reminder of the key points you will pass on this journey. It also poses more questions for you to consider as you successfully progress beyond your first year as an NQSW.

How to use this book

After three years of formal study, you know best how you learn, and therefore there is no right or wrong way to use this book. You might read the book from cover to cover, sequentially, or dip in and out of chapters, depending on where you are in terms of your professional status and/or career development. The content of each chapter provides guidance aimed at supporting you to take a proactive approach to professional development in your first year. There are reflective and practical tasks that you can adopt, or adapt, to help build a strategy for future career development during and beyond your first year.

Part I

Finding Your Feet

Throughout Part I, we focus on making the transition from student to NQSW. While you have been working towards this point for many years, the transition from student to professional can be a time of practical and emotional turmoil. This is perfectly normal and to be expected. To negotiate this phase of your professional development, Chapter 1 helps you think about the transition process and how best to manage it. Chapter 2 provides practical guidance on what is expected of you as an NQSW and the different roles individuals and organisations have in supporting you through this stage. Chapter 3 provides guidance and strategies to support you in beginning to work in your new role, highlighting the part played by induction and how to get the best from this process, as well as developing and using support mechanisms.

Chapter 1

Now I'm a Social Worker...

∴ Change and transition: from student to professional

∴ Using knowledge and experience in transition

∴ Real life, the value you can add to practice

Congratulations! If you are reading this you have either successfully completed your social work degree course, or are about to. The last pieces of formal academic work have been submitted, and placement completed. The books, journal and research papers that have been so much part of your life over the last few years sit somewhere temporarily abandoned as you sigh with relief and take the next step on your journey into practice.

As a newly qualified social worker (NQSW) in adult and mental health services, you have challenges ahead of you that are both daunting and exciting. This is a significant period in your life, a time that will be characterised by change and transition. Fortunately, this is something you have been working towards for several years so it is not unexpected or unwanted, and can be viewed as a voluntary transition (Fouad and Bynner 2008).

The fact that you have chosen this particular career path will make a difference to how you perceive your current situation (Rönkä, Oravala and Pulkkinen 2003); however, this does not mean you will not experience a range of conflicting emotions, from excitement to downright fear and anxiety, as you embark on your chosen career path. Research from allied professional groups – for example, nurses and doctors – suggests that such feelings are common for those making the journey from student to professional, as individuals reported feeling unprepared for their new role and concerned about the higher level of accountability and responsibility expected of them (Newton and McKenna 2006; Prince *et al.* 2004).

Such feelings and concerns should be considered a 'normal' reaction and part of the process of going through change and transition. However, these feelings will need to be managed, first, to reduce stress levels, and second, to support you in planning your future personal and professional development.

 At first it was scary to see oneself as a 'qualified' social worker... (NQSW)

Box 1.1 Understanding and managing change

Factors that facilitate change

- When the reasons for it are understood
- When those affected help create it
- When it follows previous successful change
- When inaugurated after prior change has been assimilated
- When planned rather than reactive

Change has occurred at different times and in different areas of your life, and it is useful to reflect on how you have managed these in the past, because it is important to be aware of how to manage the change in role from to student to qualified social worker so as to maximise the positive outcomes for you during this transition period. At a personal level change might involve moving from student accommodation back to the family home or home town, or to a new area close to your work base. Your network of support may change as friends and fellow students begin their own journeys into professional practice. This may pose particular challenges for you, although social networking sites such as Facebook and Twitter can help you to maintain those supportive relationships built up during your training. These can be very important in enabling you to share experiences and tips in surviving the ups and downs of moving from life as a student to life as a professional.

The most rewarding, and possibly daunting change, though, will be at a professional level. You are now moving into a new organisational culture where how you are perceived by others, and their expectations of you, will change dramatically once you are employed as a fully qualified practitioner (Fenge 2009). Whilst on placement you will have been 'the student'; now you will be an employee with a professional role which carries with it power and responsibility.

Donnellan and Jack (2010) suggest there are central differences that need to be understood when making the transition from student to qualified professional practitioner. As a student you were:

- accountable to your university and the lecturers and tutors who worked with you

- responsible for demonstrating an appropriate level of competence and academic ability within clear frameworks of assessment

- able to gain support and empathy from fellow students as you followed a similar pathway through higher education

- protected in the allocation of complex cases when on placement

- undertaking work experience throughout the course, which was time-limited.

Alternatively, as a qualified social worker you are:

- accountable to your employer and the social work regulatory authority in undertaking statutory duties as defined in legislation and national and local policy

- accountable for your decisions and actions

- expected to take responsibility for complex cases

- expected to demonstrate a professional level of competence in sometimes confusing and conflicting organisational systems

- one of many professionals at different stages of professional development undertaking practice.

Each role carries with it particular expectations and, as we can see, those expected of you as a qualified practitioner are somewhat different from when you were a student. Coping with, and managing, this change positively will involve a period of 'transition'. Whilst change can be related to external factors such as geographic location, living arrangements and job role, transition in this context relates to the internal processes you need to go through. Transition involves adapting the internal you, the way you respond to and cope with the cut-and-thrust of professional practice, and ultimately your cognitive and emotional responses to professional life.

Managing transition

Rather than hoping for the best it is advisable to try and understand and manage this process, as it will help reduce your anxiety levels and enable you to take control of planning your career development from the outset.

Management studies break transition down into three distinct processes, endings, in-between and new beginnings, which Bridges (1998) suggests can take six to twelve months to work through. In order to achieve transition one has to go through these phases successfully; therefore it is advisable for you to be aware of the phases, to plan how to move successfully through them.

Endings

Phase one is clearly related to successfully completing your professional qualification. This may appear a straightforward phase, but it can still present difficulties. Being known as a student has been an important part of defining who you are, as your identity has been partly expressed through your student status; it has also influenced how others see you. This is important because, whilst you may feel much the same as you did before completing your qualification, others' perceptions and expectations of you will be different because they will now view you as a professional practitioner. This will inevitably have some effect on how you feel internally and you may feel under pressure to meet those expectations. You may also experience some feelings of loss (as you leave behind student life, the familiarity of your surroundings, friends and tutors), as well as excitement at starting a new phase in your life.

In-between

This phase relates to the first stage of moving from student to professional, where academic learning may appear out of touch with the reality of practice. This phase can lead to feelings of anxiety and uncertainty, it may feel chaotic and challenging, yet ultimately it will provide the foundations on which to build your future career. Transferable skills developed whilst undertaking your degree can be utilised in the workplace to support you in this phase (Donnellan and Jack 2010), so skills such as critical analysis, reflection and reasoning should be integrated with practice experience to help you understand and develop your competence and confidence.

> **"** At first it felt like everything I had learnt at University was irrelevant, but as I became more experienced I could see it actually underpinned all I do. (NQSW) **"**

New beginnings

As you negotiate the journey through phases one and two you experience change materially, emotionally and cognitively. Your student life will now become a nostalgic memory as you begin to develop your professional identity. Professional practice, the positives and the negatives, will be part of your everyday working life. Skills and knowledge attained whilst completing your qualification are being consolidated into practice and you are planning ahead to the next stage in your professional development.

Planning and monitoring transition

Each phase will require careful planning and monitoring, if you want to make the transition from student to qualified practitioner as positive an experience as possible. Whilst social work has much to offer, it is also a complex profession. Workers can soon find themselves struggling to cope as they come to terms with meeting a range of objectives, many of which are competing, not least as you attempt to maintain your professional values in a system fraught with resourcing issues and organisational structures that seem designed to frustrate your practice. Your first year in practice will be something of a rollercoaster ride, with highs and lows. The height, depth and duration of these will depend on a variety of factors, some of which you will have control of, others not. You will need to learn to adjust and adapt to your new working environment, and this may lead to feeling somewhat deskilled at times, as you negotiate this period of transition. However, by actively planning and monitoring your progress in the first year of practice you can at least ensure that you have some element of control.

Blair (2000) provides a four-stage model you could apply to the three phases of transition to both plan and monitor your progress. The four stages consist of preparation; encounter; adjustment; and stabilisation.

Preparation

This stage relates to the changes that will need to occur to facilitate the transition from student to social worker. Fenge (2009) suggests that these can be broken down into internal and external factors.

Table 1.1 Transition: Stage 1 – preparation

Phase of transition	Stage to support transition	Action
Ending	Preparation	External – apply for jobs, re-locate, move home, open new bank account, make transport arrangements, purchase commodities to support change of role, i.e suitable clothing, briefcase, IT.
		Internal – be aware and manage change in support networks, manage feelings of loss, be aware of perception of self by others, be aware of feelings of increased/decreased confidence.
• Make a list of things you need to do to manage this phase of transition		

Encounter

This stage relates to securing your first social work position and engaging in practice as a qualified professional, as opposed to previous experience as a student.

Adjustment

This stage relates to personal, psychological and cognitive experience of change in your professional role and status.

Table 1.2 Transition: Stage 3 – adjustment

Phase of transition	Stage to support transition	Action
In-between	Encounter	What is your expectation of your new job? Relate this to induction, type of work you expect to do, the level and type of support you will receive, the quality of management and supervisory input.
	Adjustment	Review the above expectations. Are you experiencing change at a personal and professional level? Are you developing positively in your new role? Are you building supportive relationships with colleagues?

- Make a list of what you expect in your new role.
- Compare your expectations with actual experience.
- Does anything need to change?

Stabilisation

This stage relates to experiencing feelings of increased confidence and competence in undertaking your professional role.

Table 1.3 Transition: Stage 4 – stabilisation

Phase of transition	Stage to support transition	Action
New beginning	Stabilisation	You actively engage in the workplace, seeking opportunities to develop your skills and knowledge, and have a clear understanding of your role and responsibilities and the processes that facilitate practice in your organisation.

- Make a list of all the things that worried you over the past year. What is different now?
- What needs to change to advance this stage further?

Reviewing your expectations in the light of actual experience is very important in making the adjustment from student to social worker. You may feel everything is exceeding your expectations, which will give you a positive sense of professional and personal well-being. On the other hand, if your expectations have not been met, this may lead to negative feelings. At this stage of your career such feelings should be acknowledged and addressed lest they develop into something more damaging, such as apathy or burnout. If this is the case, you should ask yourself what needs to change. Do you need to adjust your expectations, or are the necessary changes related specifically to your employer?

Your concerns need to be discussed, otherwise they might lead to resentment and unhappiness on your part. You will know you have reached this phase/stage of transition when your feelings of confidence and competence in your abilities have increased, along with a clear sense of your role within your team and where you fit in and contribute to the overall effectiveness of your organisation. You will begin to feel you are practising at a level commensurate with your professional role.

The role of knowledge and experience in transition

In the first year of practice you will probably receive what might be likened to a technical apprenticeship where, as a new worker, you are inducted into a prescribed body of knowledge and skills in which you are required to become proficient (Donnellan and Jack 2010) – organisational policy and procedures, for example. However, you will also experience a period of readjustment, as knowledge that supports your practice begins to evolve. The Social Care Institute for Excellence (SCIE) (Pawson *et al.* 2003) identifies several sources of knowledge which inform the development of our knowledge, for example:

- organisational knowledge

- practitioner knowledge

- user knowledge

- research knowledge

- policy community knowledge.

SCIE goes on to suggest:

- all these sources have a vital role to play in building up the social care evidence base, there being no hierarchy suggested in the list above

- it is important not to neglect sources of knowledge that are tacit, that currently lack prestige and seem less compelling

- information needs are variable, and there is flexibility and diversity in the recommended schema in order to help individuals find appropriate evidence for their particular requirements.

(Pawson *et al.* 2003, p.viii)

Box 1.2 What knowledge do you use to support practice?

- What knowledge do you use?
- Do you prefer one source of knowledge to another?
- Does this influence the outcomes of your practice? If so, how?
- What other forms of knowledge do you need to develop?

Understanding, developing and using knowledge is central to enabling you to make progressive changes to support this transition period and to how you develop as a practitioner in your new role and meet the responsibilities and duties that are required of you by your employer and the profession's regulatory body. This period offers you important opportunities in your professional and personal developmental journey. All change involves learning, and the end of your learning at university has led to a new environment in which to learn, the workplace. The learning gained from formal education will now interact with experience attained as a qualified practitioner. You may feel the two may not always appear compatible – however, Donnellan and Jack make a pertinent point, stating: 'Both are essential to the development of competent professional practice, and bringing them together into an individually balanced equilibrium is one of the main tasks for a successful transition into the profession' (Donnellan and Jack 2010, p.36).

You will need to do this as soon as you become an employee because, regardless of the fact that you are newly qualified, the title of social worker means you will be expected to play an active role in cases that are complex and demanding, with increased levels of risk and responsibility, where you will be expected to succeed in balancing service user and carer choice and autonomy with protection in decision making.

Increasingly, social work with adults involves a variety of professional groups and organisations, and not all will agree with the decisions you make. The pressure on beds within hospital settings can lead medical professionals to seek the early discharge of service users when, in your professional opinion, you might believe this is inappropriate. You will be required to justify your professional judgement to medical practitioners who may be senior to you, such as consultants, and continue to work with them in the best interests of the service user following any disagreements.

Your knowledge, skills, and ability to communicate them to others have never been so important as now. You might therefore consider developing a plan of how to facilitate the communication and continuation of learning needed to support you in making the transition from student to social worker, not just externally but internally too. This will then help develop your competence and confidence. Competence is not just about being able to combine your skills, knowledge and experience, but, and this is even more important, being able to apply these to a given situation so that you are able to interpret what is happening and draw on a repertoire of actions to support your practice. Regardless of your training so far, it is the ability to continue in your learning and adapt it to practice that will support your transition from NQSW to confident social work practitioner to professional. Confidence is something you will need to develop if you are to manage the rigours of professional practice, and is interwoven with the development of your competence in practice.

Boshuizen, Rainer and Gruber (2004) suggest that being a professional means, in part, that you are required to take responsibility for the way you practise and for maintaining your standards. To achieve this you will now need to integrate your academic knowledge with practice experience to develop professional knowledge. Some experienced colleagues may suggest you need to leave academic learning behind because the reality of day-to-day social work practice is different and experience is the key to good practice. However, the reality is that the way you integrate formal knowledge with practice experience will be central to how you develop as a professional practitioner. Whilst it is true that you may initially discover a gap exists between academic knowledge acquired during your formal education and experience required to support everyday practice (Boshuizen *et al.* 2004; Donnellan and Jack 2010; Keen *et al.* 2009), the two are inextricably linked, and you should be aiming to better understand the complexity of the relationship between them and how they will contribute to developing a professional knowledge base in terms of their relevance and limitations. The time and energy you put into this process will depend on what calibre of practitioner you want to be in the future.

Presumably, you are aiming to be the best you possibly can and will expect to develop some level of expertise in your chosen area of specialism. Being regarded as an 'expert' will mean the people you work with, and wider society, have an expectation that you excel in your particular area of specialism (Boshuizen *et al.* 2004). This might feel a scary prospect at this moment in time; but if you were in need of professional support, who would you rather consult – someone with the right qualification, or someone who is not only qualified but regarded as possessing particular expertise in the area in which you require support? Experts are individuals who, at minimum, achieve a modicum of success in the professional role, or are viewed as excelling in their particular field.

Box 1.3 Defining an 'expert'

Can you think of someone whom you regard as an 'expert' social worker? What contributes to your understanding of this person as an expert?

Here are some of the possible reasons for your judgement:

- Advanced theoretical or subject knowledge
- Many years of experience in a particular role or area of practice
- High-level practice skills and analytic ability
- Valuable personal attributes

Source: Donnellan and Jack 2010, p.24

Studies into the strategies employed to develop expertise are useful if you want to achieve the highest level possible for you. Boshuizen *et al.* (2004) suggest it is not just about knowing more than novices, as some experienced colleagues might argue, but is also linked to how you conceptualise knowledge in a wider spectrum and structure it. This means actively making an effort to understand the relevance of academic knowledge and practice experience and how they interact and support one another to develop your professional knowledge base.

Knowledge in practice

In mental health settings, for example, whilst a consultant psychiatrist, community psychiatric nurse and social worker may have similar types of academic knowledge and practice experience to support their understanding of the possible causes of mental illness, they may conceptualise problems and solutions differently. Although certain facts and methods of intervention may be proven in research, your experience of practice from a *social work* perspective will mean you are able to include your professional knowledge in assessment and planning. This provides a world-view that is typical of your professional group and enables you to develop a distinct professional voice which may sometimes contradict that of other professionals you work with. However, it also enables you to develop responses that are person-centred, based on a holistic view of an individual, rather than a diagnostic label that can then lead to standard solutions. The purpose of integrating intellectual discipline and practice experience is more than one of assimilating learning designed to promote conformity to policy and procedure (Galpin 2009). Your aim is to be a practitioner who is critically analytical, socially aware, innovative, responsive, reflective and reflexive in practice, challenging rather than accepting of the status quo (Galpin 2009).

This relates to Lacey's (1977) model of strategies, which you might adopt to manage the transition period. The first strategy you may adopt is a 'strategic compliance' approach (Donnellan and Jack 2010, p.42), where you adhere to the requirements of the organisation you work in, even though they may conflict with your own values and beliefs – for example, when working in a hospital setting, responding to pressure from ward staff by acting to free up a bed as quickly as possible, rather than applying your preferred, person-centred approach. As you progress through transition you may find yourself achieving 'internalised adjustment' (Donnellan and Jack 2010, p.42) where you are able to voice the conflicts you experience with your peers and begin to be able to put your practice into an organisational and professional context. Finally, as you progress through your first year, 'strategic redefinition' (Donnellan and Jack 2010, p.42) characterises practice as you introduce new and creative practice.

The value you add to practice and organisations

“ Being newly qualified meant to me that I was free to ask questions, therefore I think I appeared as enthusiastic. Indeed, I feel that my enthusiasm helped to achieve better outcomes for the individuals who use services. (NQSW) **”**

Box 1.4 Real life...the value of being a 'fresh pair of eyes'

Serious Case Reviews (SCRs) are undertaken when practice goes very wrong, to try to understand what happened, and to make changes to ensure that things do not go wrong again. They are a valuable resource that can help you in your professional development. The SCR in respect of JK provides an example of the difficulties that can arise when professionals lose sight of the issues and practice becomes routine, leading to reactive rather than proactive practice.

JK was a 76-year-old woman who lived alone in rented accommodation provided by a housing association. She was reluctant to leave the home. JK had a number of health issues and there were concerns about the poor state of hygiene in the house. A number of professionals worked with JK over a sustained number of years and incidents had occurred that could have resulted in safeguarding alerts (i.e. theft and harassment in her home), but none was made.

A professional involved in her care discovered JK dead in her home in November 2008. The SCR suggests that everyone involved was clear that JK had the mental capacity to make choices. However, professionals had lost sight of how vulnerable these decisions left JK, and this had implications for professional practice.

> As a consequence, for months if not years the accepted pattern of care and support offered to her came to be reactive, dealing with the immediate concerns she raised and then withdrawing. There was a lack of multi-agency discussion about JK's situation and ownership of how to address the choices she was making. (Cornwall and Isles of Scilly Safeguarding Adults Board 2009, p.5)

The Board went on to suggest that those involved had:

> ...got confused about choice and risk. In the light of her clear and articulate resistance to receive help to change her situation, they lost the ability to work in anything but a reactive way. (p.5)

Whether new approaches are accepted will depend on the nature and structure of the organisation. However, remember you are in a unique position, bringing a 'fresh pair of eyes' to the day-to-day business in your organisation. This freshness, combined with competence and confidence, can expose the 'taken-for-grantedness' of everyday practice (Thompson 2006) where practitioners and organisations cease to question critical incidents in individuals' lives as referrals, service users and carers all merge into one and practice becomes 'routine'.

Planning ahead

Dreyfus and Dreyfus (1986) provide a useful framework for understanding where you might be, and where you want to be in the future, in terms of skills needed to develop your professional practice. All practitioners need to re-evaluate where they are in terms of skills and knowledge if they want to combat a routine approach to practice.

Table 1.4 Skills and professional practice: how might these influence practice in cases such as JK?

Skill level	Professional practice
Novice	Adherence to taught rules, decision making is limited to objective knowledge base, no discretion used.
Advanced beginner	Action guided by rules mainly, limited use of experience.
Competent	Developing ability to adapt rules in light of practice experience.
Proficient	More holistic approach; is able to identify salient points and recognise deviations from rule-based knowledge as new patterns of knowledge develop from previous experience.
Expert	Has developed an intuitive approach, no longer reliant on rigid rules, ability to apply discretion.

Table 1.4 provides only a snapshot of the stages of skills acquisition that commentators have identified as part of the process of moving from student to professional (Donnellan and Jack 2010; Dreyfus and Dreyfus 1986; Eraut 1994), and you may wish to undertake further reading to improve your understanding of the stages. Chapter 4 of this book takes a more in-depth view of how you develop your professional identity.

It should be clear to you that passing your qualifying course and being employed as a social worker does not automatically make you a professional – this requires further development...

Key considerations

- As a newly qualified social worker in adult and mental health services the challenges ahead of you are both daunting and exciting. This is a significant period in your life, a time that will be characterised by change and transition.

- Change will occur at a personal and professional level, leading to developing new and/or existing support networks as you make the transition from student to professional.

- Transition involves adapting the internal you, the way you respond to and cope with the cut-and-thrust of professional practice, and ultimately your cognitive and emotional responses to professional life.

- Understanding, developing and using knowledge is central to enabling you to make progressive changes to support this transition period and the way you develop as a practitioner in your new role and meet the responsibilities and duties required of you by your employer and the profession's regulatory body.

- Confidence is something you need to develop if you are to manage the rigours of professional practice, and is interwoven with the development of your competence in practice.

- Passing your qualifying programme and being employed in a social work role does not automatically make you a professional – this requires further development.

- Your ability to view practice with a fresh pair of eyes can challenge the status quo and lead to better outcomes for those who use the service.

Chapter 2

Understanding and Using NQSW Status

- NQSW frameworks that support your first year in practice
- Making it work for you
- What can I do now to prepare for NQSW?

Engaging in, and managing, transition and change is clearly a key element in your professional development. A crucial next step in this process involves you becoming an NQSW for your first year in practice. This is a relatively new development for those entering adult and mental health services; NQSW frameworks and status have been piloted first within children's services. The adults frameworks will provide the foundation of any induction programme your employer offers you. (Induction is discussed in more depth in Chapter 3.)

The shape and form of your first year in practice will depend, in some part, on where you are registered as a social worker. The United Kingdom is divided into four different countries: England, Wales, Northern Ireland and Scotland, and each has its own regulatory council and guidance on how NQSWs should be supported as they embark on their social work career. Therefore, where you are registered, and the country you work in, will make a difference to what support you can expect to receive from your employer in your first year of practice, and beyond.

No matter which country you practise in, the purpose of the NQSW frameworks are twofold: first, to ensure that as an NQSW you are safe to practise as a competent, capable and responsible practitioner; and second, to ensure that employers provide appropriate professional support. As with many areas in the public sector, social work requirements and regulations are evolving all of the time, often in response to wider socio-political and economic challenges. Therefore, you will need to ensure that you are aware of the current regulatory requirements for NQSWs in your country. To do this you need to know who your regulatory body is and what their professional requirements are (see Appendix I for guidance).

The purpose of NQSW frameworks

> The NQSW framework is based on good practice and provides a bridge between your qualifying training and your employment in adult services. (Skills for Care 2009, p.7)

It has been recognised that the first year of practice is a critical period in your professional development and that a formal programme of support is of great value (SWRB 2010). As such, any requirements you have to meet should provide a framework for your induction into your new job. (Induction and starting work in a new organisation are discussed in more depth in Chapter 3.)

The aim of all the frameworks is to support you in developing your skills, competence and confidence in a systematic way during your first year in practice by providing you with focused supervision, support and guidance. Donnellan and Jack (2010) suggest NQSW frameworks provide an apprenticeship model where you will be inducted into the workplace to ensure that you meet the organisation's procedural needs using 'a clearly defined set of knowledge and skills' (p.30) that are passed onto you by a senior colleague. Whilst this sounds positive, an evaluation of the first NQSW pilot schemes in English children's services suggests there can be variations in the application of NQSW status, with 40 per cent of NQSWs reporting that they were unhappy with their programmes (Community Care 2010a). It is wise to be under no illusions – whilst such a framework provides clear guidance, how it is interpreted and implemented in the workplace will make the difference between a positive and negative first year in practice, and this may vary from employer to employer.

" The programme was initially disorganised in terms of arrangement by my agency...but eventually issues were addressed. (NQSW) **"**

The commitment a potential employer demonstrates to an NQSW framework may well be an indication of the level of support you are likely to receive from them, so, if you have the luxury of choosing an employer, this might be one factor to take into consideration before accepting an offer of employment. However, the reality for you might be that you have no choice but to accept an offer of employment regardless of the employer's commitment to the NQSW framework. In this event it still provides a useful guide on how to structure your first year in practice. The development of all the frameworks is based on research, which has identified the best way to support students in making a safe transition from student to professional social worker. Therefore, it has much to offer you as an NQSW in terms of making the transition from student to professional.

Making NQSW status work for you

At interview it would be appropriate to ask what arrangements will be made to support you as an NQSW. For example what management, support and development can you expect in your first year? How will mentoring and supervisory arrangements be organised? How will your case and workload be protected? Whilst you will have a larger and more complex caseload than when you were a student, for an NQSW the quantity of work should take into consideration time for CPD activities – for example, in Wales the Welsh Assembly Government recommends that one day per month is provided to implement your development plan (Care Council for Wales 2008a).

The answers you receive to these types of questions are very important, as they will give you an indication of your potential employer's commitment to you as an NQSW. If you are in a position to choose who to work for, you might opt for the employer with the most progressive and proactive system in place. However, you may need to accept a post even if the answers to the above questions are not as good as you would like, and in such cases remember that guidance as outlined above still provides a plan to work with to ensure that your first year in practice is as positive as possible. This could then be used within the supervisory process to plan your future career development. (Chapter 6 provides more detailed guidance on how to make best use of supervisory arrangements.)

Box 2.1 Using the NQSW framework in the interview process

In preparation for your interview, become familiar with the requirements for both you and your potential employer under the relevant NQSW framework. Questions you might ask at interview could include:

- Will I be recognised as an NQSW?
- If so, what arrangements are in place to support me as an NQSW?
- How will you be supported to meet the requirements of the appropriate NQSW framework? (For example, caseload allocation, supervisory/ mentoring arrangements, time to engage in CPD/PRTL activity.)
- What types of CPD/PRTL activity will be made available to me?
- If there are any issues during the NQSW period, how will these be addressed and by whom?

Before attending an interview, think what answers you would expect to these questions, knowing what you know about the employer's responsibilities under the NQSW framework, and write down what the key points are for you. Following interview, compare the potential employer's answers with what you expected. How do they compare? How do you feel about this – concerned or reassured?

Regardless of which framework you might fall under, there is a requirement that as an NQSW you take responsibility for your professional development, although this should be viewed in the context of a partnership between you and your employer – for example, working with your employer to identify training and developmental objectives, being proactive in arranging and participating in supervision, engaging in employer induction programmes and attending learning events developed to support you (Chapters 3, 6 and 8 provide further guidance on how you might facilitate this).

As an NQSW you will also be responsible for ensuring that you collate any evidence that supports you in demonstrating that you have met any professional requirements contained within the NQSW framework – for example, outcome statements in England, or the requirements of Assessed Year in Employment (AYE)/Assessed and Supported Year in Employment (ASYE) in Northern Ireland and England, or Post-Registration Training and Learning (PRTL) in Wales and Scotland – linked to your professional registration. How this is evidenced will need to be agreed between you, your employer, your supervisor and your regulatory body. You may be required to complete a Record of Achievement (Scotland), Personal Development Plan (Northern Ireland) or Transitional Personal Development Planning tool (England).

Whichever framework you work to, they all offer opportunities that you can utilise to support you in the transition from student to professional in the first year of practice, and which will provide a foundation for your second year in practice and beyond, in terms of CPD (which is discussed more fully in Chapter 8).

It cannot be reiterated enough that use of such frameworks is essential in the first year of practice, as they can help you make sense of your personal and professional development, and ultimately provide a sound foundation for your future. Throughout your career you will be expected to take responsibility in planning your professional development and keeping up to date with the knowledge, skills and abilities relevant to social work practice (Skills for Care 2009), so it is advisable to begin thinking and planning at the earliest opportunity.

Why an NQSW framework is important for you

- Good quality support to NQSWs improves confidence and readiness to practise.

- Access to a structured induction process improves workers' understanding of their role.

- Appropriate supervision supports effective, safe practice.

- Good quality professional development opportunities support improved recruitment and retention of workers.

What can I do now to prepare for being an NQSW?

Donnellan and Jack (2010) rightly suggest, in the context of preparing for practice, that individuals new to a profession realise that 'learning comes through doing' (p.38), but it is also useful to remember you are not entering the profession as an NQSW with no life or practice experience at all. In preparation for formal training you may have undertaken some voluntary work, or have been employed in the social care sector for many years. Your time in placements during your qualifying programme will have also provided you with some ideas about what practice might be like, which skills you used to thrive and pass the placement, and which skills and knowledge you need to develop. These experiences are a useful source of information that you can utilise as a prospective NQSW, which could prove useful in two ways: first, to reflect on your developmental journey so far, which will build your confidence; and second, to learn from how you have managed certain situations in the past. Whether those have been positive or negative experiences, you can learn something from them, and this learning can help inform your developmental needs as an NQSW (this is discussed in further depth in Chapter 3).

NQSW, learning and professional development

> Learning one set of skills at school, technical college or university is no longer enough to carry people through their working life. But there is one basic skill that is becoming increasingly important in today's fast-changing technological universe: being able to learn and adapt to the new skills and training that will be required. (Organisation for Economic Co-operation and Development (OECD) 2007)

A useful starting point from which to prepare for your role as an NQSW would be to collate evidence of such learning and start to develop your own personal record of professional development. Box 2.2 offers a pro forma you might use.

Box 2.2 Pro forma for your personal record of professional development

Key learning experience

- What happened?
- Who was involved?

Reflection

- How did you feel?
- What tensions or conflicts emerged during this piece of work?
- What knowledge and skills did you use to manage this situation?
- Were there any issues of discrimination and oppression and were you able to resolve these? If so, how?
- What would you have liked the outcome to look like, or do you feel the outcome was good enough?

Learning for the future

- What worked?
- What did not work?
- What do you think would support your professional development in the future?

Key considerations

- The United Kingdom is divided into four different countries: England, Wales, Northern Ireland and Scotland, and each has its own regulatory council and guidance on how newly qualified social workers should be supported as they embark on their social work career.

- Regardless of which framework you might fall under, there is a requirement that as an NQSW you take responsibility for your professional development, although this should be viewed in the context of a partnership between you and your employer.

- Reflecting on your previous experiences of practice, prior to becoming an NQSW, may help you determine your focus in the first year of practice.

Chapter 3

Starting Work in a New Organisation

∴ Preparing for starting work in a new organisation

∴ Preparing for your new role

∴ The induction process

∴ Learning about resources that support professional practice

The transition from student to professional has already been considered in Chapter 1 and it is clear that entering the workforce for the first time and making the transition from student to qualified practitioner can be stressful and unsettling, raising feelings of uncertainty and being unprepared (Fenge 2009; Newton and McKenna 2006; Schrader 2008). However, it is important to recognise that, regardless of professional status and experience as a practitioner, starting work in a new organisation at any time in your career is extremely anxiety-provoking and therefore *preparation* is a key element that can assist the transition, whether it is within a new organisation or a new working environment. This chapter focuses on the different elements of preparation that can support this process.

> Although the final stages of your social work training and practice placements facilitate the transition from student to social worker, the final stage of transition from student to social worker occurs after you begin employment. (Koerin, Harrigan and Reeves 1990)

Preparing for practice: induction standards and NQSW frameworks

The NQSW frameworks in the UK recognise the support that people starting out in the social work profession need, and this includes a good quality induction both to the profession *and* to the organisation that you are working for (Skills for Care 2009).

It is important, therefore, to differentiate between different types of 'induction'. This chapter will look at formal induction to a new workplace and specific job induction as a new worker, as well as induction to professional practice and developing professional competence.

First, it is important to highlight the introduction of induction standards/frameworks across the UK – for example, the 'common induction standards' (CIS) in England (Skills for Care 2010a), which provide eight standards (see Appendix II) for all people either entering social care or changing roles, or employers within adult social care. They are designed to be met within a 12-week period and are to ensure that all new workers are supported through a thorough induction period, the idea being that the CIS should complement the NQSW framework and not result in duplication of evidence.

It is important to find out how your employer uses these standards alongside the NQSW framework, and (if you work outside of England) how induction frameworks are linked into the NQSW framework. See:

- Northern Ireland Social Care Council – *Induction Standards NI: Standards for New Workers in Social Care* (2007), Appendix II.

- Care Council for Wales – *Social Care Induction Framework for Wales* (2008b), Appendix II.

- Scottish Social Services Council – *Preparing for Practice – Induction Guidance for Social Service Employers in Scotland* (2011), Appendix II.

Induction frameworks can be used as a tool to audit and review the skills, knowledge and experience of new staff and assist in identifying development needs (Care Council for Wales 2008b).

Preparing for starting work in a new organisation

Odro, Vlancy and Foster (2010) considered the transition from student to qualified worker for nurses, and found that one of the most consistent messages from research was 'reality shock' (Kramer 1974) when starting out on their career – for example, thinking that they were prepared for professional practice, but finding they actually were not. This was true not just for people new to the profession, but also for experienced practitioners moving across specialist areas.

Research looking at a variety of health professionals' transition from student to professional has found common early experiences of uncertainty, lack of confidence, inadequate role preparation and inadequate knowledge (Gerrish 2001; Odro et al. 2010; Prince et al. 2004).

All of this highlights the importance of good preparation and a good induction process to support you in dealing with your uncertainties and anxieties and in developing the knowledge and skill base that you will need to undertake your new role. Research also shows that structured support during this transition period is needed (Delaney 2003; Odro et al. 2010).

We shall explore formal induction policies and processes later in the chapter, but here it is relevant to say that some key elements of the induction process and introduction to a new job start when you apply for the job and when you are interviewed for the post (e.g. information provided within the application pack and information provided at interview). Consequently, before your first day you have actually already gathered quite a lot of information that could support you to feel less anxious and more prepared (see the exercise below). If you have yet to apply for a post, then thinking about the information that you need from the application and interview stage is important and can assist you when you start the new job.

Alongside the information you may have already gathered, some initial preparation before your first day will help you organise yourself and reduce some of the anxiety you may feel on your first day. The more information you have, the more prepared you will feel and this should make you a bit less anxious.

Box 3.1 Exercise: Initial preparation

What information have you already got (or can get) that will facilitate your transition into your new job?

Application

- What information was provided in the job application pack?
- What does the job description say, e.g. key roles and responsibilities?
- Have you been provided with any information about the organisation, e.g. structure of wider organisation, different agencies and teams?
- Aims/objectives/ethos of the organisation.

Interview

- What information did you gather at interview about the organisation, office and role?
- Did the questions you were asked during your interview provide you with any information about the organisation/agency/team priorities?
- What questions did you ask (can you ask) to gain a better understanding of the organisation and role?

Job offer letter

- Was any information included about terms and conditions of employment, pay, annual leave, sickness policy, grievance policy, pension, appraisal, probationary periods, etc?

The first day in any job can be overwhelming, and you are likely to meet a lot of people and be provided with a lot of information that you will never be able to remember. It can be really useful to take a notebook with you, so that you can jot down useful information as people tell you and then refer back to it later in the evening as you try to make sense of things.

It is important to remember that your first day is just that – it's a beginning and you do not need to find out everything and meet everyone. Some things are more important to find out straightaway and other things will be part of a longer process of induction and introduction. Again, planning and preparation is therefore important and having a think about the main information you will want to gather on your first day may be useful.

Box 3.2 Exercise: Things to find out before your first day

1. Make contact with your line manager/the point of contact you have been provided with and find out the following things:

- What time should you arrive on day one?
- What are the car parking arrangements?
- Who will be there on your first day to meet you?
- Is there a dress code that you need to be aware of?
- Are there any security arrangements you need to be aware of (e.g for the front door or car park)?

2. Think about how long it will take you to get to work – ensure that you allow for the time of day and traffic, and remember that when you attended for interview it may have been a different time of day.

- It may be worth having a practice run at the same time of day.

3. Get to know the local area.

- Drive around/familiarise yourself with the main routes around your patch.
- Get a good street map.

Box 3.3 Exercise: What do you need to find out on your first day?

Health and safety factors

- Fire exits/fire alarms, etc.
- Mobile phone – personal safety/lone working policy.
- Signing in and out procedures/whereabouts board.

Comfort factors

- Location of toilets and tea and coffee facilities.
- Where to leave personal belongings.

Admin issues

- Administrators – who are they/what do they do?
- Access to computer/IT support.
- Access to telephone/key numbers.
- Post/in-trays.

Important people

- Who is based where?
- Telephone numbers and contact details.

Preparing for your new role

Box 3.4 Exercise: Initial preparation for your new role

- Reflect on the core social work values, knowledge and skills that you are bringing with you from your social work training – how will these help you in your new role?

- Make a list of your strengths that you and/or others have identified during your social work training (or previous post), and think about how these will contribute to your new team and work with service users.

- What experiences have you had that help prepare you for this new role (e.g. pre-social work training employment, social work training placements, personal situations)?

- Go back over the information you have already gathered about the new role and/or organisation you are going to be working in (see previous exercises) and reflect upon the organisation's aims and ethos and where you will fit into this with the experience, knowledge, skills and values that you bring.

- What knowledge have you already gained from your social work training that you can revise/refresh to help you prepare for your new role (e.g. legal frameworks, General Social Care Council's (GSCC) code of practice (General Social Care Council 2004), The British Association of Social Workers' (BASW) *The Code of Ethics for Social Work* (The British Association of Social Workers 2002), core social work theories that can inform your practice, etc.)?

Later in this chapter we will think about your role-related induction, specifically the information, knowledge and skills you will need to gain and develop in relation to your new role. However, there is some preparation that you can do before starting your new job. Even though you may feel like there is a whole list of things you need to learn on starting a new job, it is also important to reflect on areas of existing experience, knowledge, skills and values, and to recognise the strengths that you will be bringing to your new post and how these can translate into your new role. Think about the knowledge base that you may need for your new role and see if there is any initial preparatory reading you could undertake before starting your new job, as this may help you to feel more prepared.

The following two scenarios may help you think about how you can prepare for your new role and reflect on the experience, knowledge, skills and values you will be bringing with you into your new role.

Scenario 1: Jay

Jay has just finished his social work training and secured a job as a social worker in a learning disabilities team. Before starting his social work training Jay worked for two years as a support worker for people with learning disabilities in a group home. Jay therefore has lots of previous experience of working with people with learning disabilities, which will assist him in his new role.

During his social work training Jay had his first placement in a hostel for individuals who are homeless, where, although this work experience was not specific to people with learning disabilities, Jay developed a knowledge and skill base that will be useful in many ways. Jay's second placement during his social work training was in a physical disabilities social work team, which again has provided him with some core knowledge, skills and values that he can take forward into his new role.

In particular, Jay can reflect on the following areas in preparation for his new role:

- His previous experience of working with people with learning disabilities enabled him to develop skills and knowledge in relation to communication needs, different methods of communicating, listening and advocacy skills, working with carers and families, etc.

- His previous social work placement within the hostel provided experience in elements of multi-agency working, information sharing, needs and risk assessment. Jay has also developed a working knowledge of the benefits and housing system, which will be useful for his future role. Jay used this placement as an opportunity to reflect on his value base and the conflicts that can often arise in practice, i.e. balancing service user wishes and choice with risks and need for protection.

- Jay's previous social work placement within a physical disabilities team enabled him to gain valuable experience of the care management process, in particular assessing service user needs, developing care plans, applying for funding and purchasing services, all of which will be part of his new role too. During this placement Jay also had to work closely with a range of other professionals, e.g. occupational therapists, physiotherapists and voluntary organisations, which again will play an important part in his new role.

- In preparation for his new role as a social worker for people with learning disabilities Jay has been reading up/refreshing himself around the key pieces of legislation and policy that he feels may be useful (e.g. Mental Capacity Act 2005; the NHS and Community Care Act 1990; Community Care (Direct Payments) Act 1996; Carers (Recognition and Services) Act 1995; Carers and Disabled Children Act 2004; *Valuing People* (Cm 5086 2001); *Valuing People Now* (Department of Health 2009c)), all of which he studied during his training.

- Jay has also spent some time reflecting on the principles of 'normalisation' and 'social role valorisation' (Wolfensberger 1972, 1983), which he feels underpin many approaches to working with people with learning disabilities. He has also thought about the social model of disability and how this will fit with his new role.

Scenario 2: Vicky

Vicky has just finished her final social work placement within an older persons' social work team. Her previous placement was for a voluntary organisation at a drop-in centre for people with mental health problems, and Vicky also has previous work experience as a support worker for people with mental health problems. She now has a new job as a social worker within a community mental health team (CMHT) and can reflect on the following areas in preparation for her new role:

- Vicky has substantial practical experience of working with people with mental health problems, and therefore can reflect on her experiences and knowledge of the impact of mental ill-health on individuals, their families and their carers. She can give some thought to the oppression and stigma that people with mental illness experience and how she will address this as a social worker.

- As a social worker within a CMHT Vicky will need to have an understanding of the different models of mental disorder (i.e. the medical model *vs* the social model) and how these will inform her practice. Vicky can familiarise herself with the various diagnosis/classifications of mental disorder (see DSM-IV (APA 2001)/ICD-10 (WHO 1992)), since, although she will not be directly involved in diagnosing mental disorder, she will need to have an understanding of the language used by professionals and the impact such diagnostic labels might have on the individual. Vicky will also need to reflect on the different treatment available (e.g. medication, ECT and psychological therapies) and how these interact with the social work role.

- Vicky can use her previous experience within an older persons' social work team to reflect on the social work role and the similarities and differences compared to a CMHT, e.g. her role in assessment and care planning, risk assessment, advocacy, carers support, mobilising resources, etc.

- Vicky can undertake some preparatory reading/refreshing around the legal and policy context that she will be working within (e.g. Mental Health Act 1983 (amended 2007); Mental Capacity Act 2005; *Deprivation of Liberty Safeguards* (Ministry of Justice 2009); Care Programme Approach (CPA) (Department of Health 1990); and *Refocusing the Care Programme Approach* (Department of Health 2008b); *National Service Framework* (Department of Health 1999), etc.) and reflect on how these underpin her new role.

- Vicky can reflect upon her role in assessing and managing risk – it may be useful to do some preparatory reading around risk assessment processes and think about some of the dilemmas she may face in terms of managing risks, whilst also promoting choice and independence.

The induction process
What is an induction?

Induction is the process which helps new members…settle into the organisation and their new job, but established staff also need an induction to any new roles they take on. (Hafford-Letchfield *et al.* 2008, p.118)

The aim of an induction is not just to help you settle into the new environment, but also to ensure that you have an adequate knowledge of the workplace and the roles and responsibilities required of you to undertake your job. A study of newly qualified social workers in 2006 found that just fewer than three-quarters had some form of workplace induction; however, few were provided with a formal, structured and managed induction process (Bates *et al.* 2010).

Hafford-Letchfield *et al.* (2008) state that induction is more than just providing an 'induction pack' and should include:

- consideration of past experiences, skills and knowledge that you bring and how they translate into your new job

- consideration of the areas of learning and development needed and how these can be achieved (CPD)

- consideration of support needs and useful support networks.

Box 3.5 What induction does your organisation or agency provide?

- Is there a written induction policy within your organisation/agency/team?
- How can you get a copy?
- Who else is involved in your induction (e.g. line manager, supervisor, buddy)?

Whilst there may be a formal induction policy, it is important to recognise that the induction process must support your own professional development. You have a responsibility to ensure that it meets this, so the process may require adjusting to tailor it to your professional needs (Bradley 2006; Gray 2009).

Using supervision to review the induction process and whether it is meeting, or has met, your needs is important. Although the formal workplace induction may only be structured for two to six weeks, your induction to the profession should be conducted over the first 12 months, and therefore ongoing review is vital (see Chapter 8 on supervision and how you can use it to support your development).

Types of induction

Donnellan and Jack (2010) distinguish three separate types of induction:

1. *Workplace induction*: specific to an actual workplace or office.

2. *Corporate induction*: concerning the wider organisation, where you and your agency or team fit into this, and issues common to all staff starting in the organisation.

3. *Role-related induction*: knowledge specific to the role, key forms and reports.

1. WORKPLACE INDUCTION

We covered a lot of the practical preparation that you can undertake before the first day of a new job at the beginning of this chapter. However, it is also useful to think about your workplace and immediate team and identify where you fit into the bigger picture.

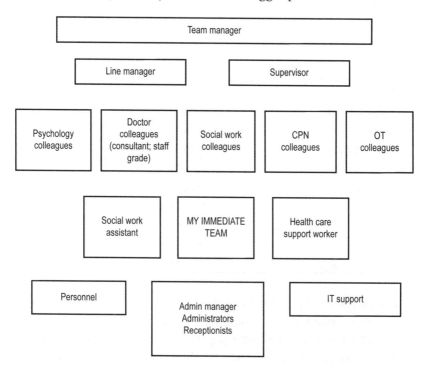

Figure 3.1 An example of a workplace chart for a Community Mental Health Team

Creating a map or chart of the key figures within your team (see example in Figure 3.1) can be a useful way of remembering people, and who you need to arrange to spend time with or contact as part of the induction process. You can add names and contact details to the map or chart if you wish, as you find out this information.

You can develop additional maps or charts of the other teams and partnership agencies that you will be working closely with. This will help you identify who you need to contact and visit as part of your induction. Table 3.1 provides examples of the partnership agencies that you might include in your charts if you are based in a mental health or adult social work setting.

Table 3.1 Partnership chart for a mental health or adult social work setting

Partner teams in a mental health setting	Partner teams in adult services
Other local CMHTs	GP practices/district nurses
Assertive outreach team	Personal assistant provision
Crisis intervention team	Community services
Home treatment team	Residential provision
In-patient services	Day-care services
Early intervention service	Transport services
Child and Adolescent Mental Health Service (CAMHS)	Respite care provision
Housing department	In-patient services/wards
Benefits agency	Carers' provision
Voluntary organisations	Community Mental Health Team (CMHT)
Rehabilitation services	Voluntary organisations
GP practices	Housing
Perinatal care	Physiotherapy
Drug and alcohol services	Occupational therapy
Police	Benefits agency
Psychological services	Psychological services

It is important to use the time during your induction period to gather as much information as possible about the partnership agencies and services that you may link into (e.g. what are their eligibility criteria, and how do you make a referral?). Think about how you are going to introduce yourself and your role to the key people – should you arrange a visit and maybe spend some time in the other team to find out how they work, or will a phone call or introductory email be sufficient?

Box 3.6 Exercise: Getting to know your workplace and partners

- Complete maps or charts for the central figures in your own workplace and partnership agencies/teams/services.
- Include contact details for the central figures.
- Request information about eligibility criteria and referral procedures for the partnership agencies.
- Arrange visits or introductory contact as necessary.
- Think about: What do I bring to this team? Where do I fit into the wider teams and services?

---

2. CORPORATE INDUCTION

It is important to find out whether there is a corporate induction programme or a formal introduction to the wider organisation. This is often arranged by the training department and deals with the issues that are common to all staff within the organisation (e.g. ethos of the organisation, future plans for the organisation, personnel and human resources issues, IT systems and support services).

It is important to reflect on where you and your immediate team fit into the wider organisation, and it is useful to gain a broader understanding of what the organisation is trying to achieve by looking at its business plans and strategies (Gray 2009).

Box 3.7 Exercise: Introduction to the wider organisation

- Develop an organisational structure chart or map for the wider organisation. Identify the key departments within the organisation and the key people within these departments. You may need to do a few different charts and show linkages across the departments and teams.
- Reflect on where your team and/or department fits into the wider organisational structure – familiarise yourself with the organisational ethos, business plan and any strategies in place for future development.

---

3. ROLE-RELATED INDUCTION

Alongside the practical elements of getting to know your team and wider services and procedures, you will need a period of introduction and learning around your role, role-related tasks and responsibilities, and key policies and procedures that will support your role, as well as an introduction to your caseload and how your caseload will be managed and supervised.

We have reflected above on the preparation you may already have been able to do in relation to your new role, and the following sections of the chapter will now build on this.

Why it is important to have a good knowledge of the law and policy guidance

The relevant legal and policy framework outlines your legal duties and responsibilities and provides a framework for your decision making in practice. Cree and Wallace (2009) highlight that legislation shapes and determines what social workers do and provides the starting point when considering risk and protection. They stress that the onus is on social workers to familiarise themselves with the applicable legislation and procedures that will come into play. It is therefore vital that you have a clear understanding of the legislation and policy that underpins your role and are able to apply it to practice (this is discussed in more depth in Chapter 5). Initially you could use supervision to reflect on the application of law and policy in practice situations.

Box 3.8 Exercise: Key legislation, policy and procedures that support your role

- Make a list of the key pieces of legislation and policy that support your role. (See Appendix III for examples of some of the main legislation and policy documents for those working with adult services – but please note that this is just a guide for a few of the important pieces and not an exhaustive list.)

- Make a list of the procedures that you will need to follow, and build up a folder of the written policies and paperwork that you will need for your role, for example:

  o   assessment procedures and forms

  o   risk assessment policy and forms

  o   care plans

  o   funding request procedures and forms

  o   referral forms

  o   case recording procedures.

A role-related induction includes thinking about opportunities for shadowing and co-working. The NQSW framework in England (Skills for Care 2009) places responsibility on the professional supervisor to consider where shadowing is appropriate, and also to provide examples of high-quality written work where required. It is therefore important for you to think about whom it would be useful to shadow, and to discuss this at an early stage with your supervisor.

A reduced and protected caseload

It is also important to find out what is in place to help you slowly build up your caseload over time, and to find out if there are any opportunities to joint work some cases as part of the induction process. Skills for Care (2010a) suggests that one of the main roles of the professional supervisor for an NQSW is to ensure that work is allocated properly; that caseloads are appropriate and managed; and that work is assigned at the level of complexity that fits your experience and is consistent with any transitional development plan you have in place (Skills for Care 2010a). You may need to be proactive here, as a report considering the impact of the NQSW framework in adult services in England (Skills for Care 2011) suggests that this is an area where progress is still needed, with protected development time being inadequate and some NQSWs stating that they were not allowed any protected development time. Many also stated that their level of experience was not taken into account (or only to a limited extent) when allocating cases. You have a key role in ensuring that you have an appropriately managed caseload, so it is important for you to reflect on how you will ensure that this happens in practice and to consider it early on in the induction process.

Developing key skills

Bates et al. (2010) found in their study of NQSWs that about one quarter of the sample did not feel prepared in some important areas of practice (e.g. assessments and report writing), and some of those studied commented that it would have been useful to have had templates or past reports to look at.

Box 3.9 Exercise: Gathering practice tools

- Gather a variety of completed assessments and reports from a range of different practitioners – e.g. core assessments, risk assessments, court reports, tribunal reports, requests for funding, care plans, carers' assessments, review forms, etc.

- Reflect on the style of the assessment or report. How does this fit with your own style? Are there any examples of good practice that you can take forward into your own work? What would you do differently?

- Allocate time to discuss the above in a supervision session.

Professional relationships and multi-agency working

Earlier in the chapter we looked at the importance of introducing yourself to your colleagues and partner agencies and developing good relationships and links. Alongside the need for introductions and identifying key contacts is the need to develop a good understanding of others' roles and to reflect on the ways that you will need to work together and some of the challenges that you will face.

Herald and Lymbery (2002) looked at the role of the social worker within multi-disciplinary learning disability services. They found that it is important to reflect on the social work contribution to the team in terms of values, knowledge and skill base, besides thinking about how others perceive the role of the social worker.

Box 3.10 Exercise: Introduction to multidisciplinary/multi-agency working

- What are your main roles and responsibilities? Use your job description, legal framework, local policies, and practice guidance to determine these.

- Ask your colleagues from other professional backgrounds what they feel your main role and responsibilities are. Compare their answers with your own view.

- What do you understand are the main role and responsibilities of your colleagues from different disciplines? Compare your own views with them directly.

- Allocate time within supervision to discuss the above with your supervisor and to reflect on the social work role within the team and wider agencies.

In order to reflect upon the social work contribution, it is also important to have a good knowledge of the role and responsibilities of your colleagues from other professions.

In preparing for practice and multi-agency working it is important to look at how information is recorded within your team and to reflect on information-sharing processes across agencies, and on some of the issues you may face. As part of your induction it is important for you to look at the policies and procedures around case recording and information-sharing. There are many examples of serious case reviews and inquiries that have examined deaths or serious incidents involving service users (both children and adult cases) where information-recording, information-sharing and multi-agency communication have been highlighted as poor and needing improvement. Therefore this is an area that you should focus on right from the outset of your career.

Box 3.11 Exercise: Introduction to recording and sharing information

- Are there formal written policies on recording case information and sharing information across agencies? Discuss within supervision.

- Gather examples of case recordings from your colleagues. What information are they recording, and how? Discuss within supervision and reflect on your own style.

- Reflect on why clear case recording is important. Think about the types of situations where your case recordings may be used by other professionals and agencies and what sort of information will need to be shared. Discuss in supervision.

- Learn from inquiries. Do some useful reading around inquiry reports, recommendations around recording and sharing of information, and multi-agency working, for example:

  o 'Findings of reviews into care and treatment of 21 mental health patients – February 2010' (NHS London 2010).

  o The Protection of Children in England: A Progress Report (Laming 2009).

  o 'The Murder of Steven Hoskin. A Serious Case Review' (Cornwall Adult Protection Committee 2007).

  o 'The Victoria Climbié Inquiry, Report of an Inquiry by Lord Laming' (Laming 2003).

  o 'The Report of the Inquiry into the Care and Treatment of Christopher Clunis' (Ritchie et al. 1994).

Learning about resources that support professional practice

It will not be a surprise to hear that social work practice is at times stressful (Collins 2008) and that people leave the profession for a variety of reasons that include workload pressures, lack of support, lack of supervision, frustration and powerlessness in the working environment (Collins 2008; Howe 2009; Huxley *et al.* 2005). It is therefore a vital part of the induction and preparation for practice process to reflect on your support needs and to find out what resources are available to support professional practice. (Support networks will be considered in more detail in Chapter 7.)

It may be useful to think about support in the following categories.

Employment support

- *Human resources policies*: pay, leave, pension, appraisal, probationary period details, etc., can all be really important features of your ongoing employment, and therefore you need to make sure that you have all the relevant information from the start. For example, what is the process for taking time off for any additional hours worked? This is going to be really important once you have had to stay late at work on a few occasions. How do you claim travel expenses? What can you claim?

- *Welfare services and employment support*: occupational health, counselling services, advice lines, trade union membership and professional body membership (e.g. the British Association of Social Workers (BASW)) are also important considerations.

- *Training courses*: is there a formal process for booking onto training? Who needs to agree this? Is there an annual training diary or programme?

Role-related support

- *Supervision*: what is the supervision policy (see Chapter 8)? How often will you get formal supervision? What is supervision used for? What methods of informal/group supervision are available?

- *Buddy system or mentors*: are you allocated a buddy or mentor to support you through the initial stages? Are mentors used at any other developmental stages?

- *Colleagues/team members*: as you get to know your colleagues you will decide which people you get on best with and who you can approach for different aspects of support, e.g. in the initial stages who do you feel comfortable asking where to find things? Who can you approach to shadow/co-work? Are there any colleagues who have also recently joined the team and can therefore offer reassurance and advice at this time?

- *Team meetings/forums*: how is the team meeting used to provide support to your role? Are there any other forums that may be of use to you within the wider organisation?

Key considerations

- The transition from student to practitioner, starting a new job in a new organisation or changing your role is an anxious time. However, good preparation and planning will assist you in making this transition.

- Gathering information is an important aspect of the induction stage – about your role, your team, your workplace, your wider organisation. It is important to be clear about where you and your team fit into the wider organisation and about the main links to other agencies.

- Identify key contacts and introduce yourself and your role to colleagues and other partner agencies. Find out as much as you can about other people's roles and responsibilities.

- It is important to reflect on your existing knowledge, skills and values and how these can be translated into your new role. This will help you to identify the areas of knowledge and learning that you need to develop.

- Shadowing and co-working opportunities are important and should form a key part of your induction to assist you to understand your role and the processes that underpin it.

- There are many important resources that back up your employment and support you in your new role. It is important to find out about these and how to access them.

Part II

Finding Your Way

In Part II, we move on from taking the initial step from student to professional to focus on life as a qualified professional. Central to this process will be the need to develop your understanding of your professional identity.

Social work with adults occurs within a variety of professional settings, in both the statutory and non-statutory sectors and alongside a variety of professional groups. It is important for you to develop a clear understanding of different professional roles and a strong sense of your own professional identity in order to know how you fit into the broader context of health and social care settings. Understanding who you are and what makes you different from other professionals is the first step towards developing your professional identity and will provide a foundation on which to build your knowledge and skills and develop your professional practice.

Having begun to develop your professional identity you will also need to develop a clear understanding of the roles and tasks you will be expected to undertake in your professional role. Chapter 4 provides a framework for developing your understanding of the expectations that there will be of you and what shapes these. Once you begin to develop your professional identity and understand these expectations, you will also need to consider how to maintain your motivation in a profession that can be challenging and demanding. The latter part of Chapter 4 provides some guidance on developing and maintaining motivation in the longer term.

Chapter 5 focuses on defining the professional role and tasks, exploring factors that shape these and tensions you might encounter in trying to meet them. The second part of the chapter identifies the importance of maintaining motivation in developing skills and knowledge to undertake the professional role and tasks associated with it.

Chapter 4

Developing My Professional Identity...

* The current context of the social work profession and how it has developed

* What it means to be a professional

* Professional knowledge

* Role of the regulatory bodies

* Codes of conduct

* Social work values and ethics

In Chapter 1, we explored the transition process from student to professional. In this chapter we will look in more detail at what this really means for you. What does it mean to be a professional? You have achieved the first stage of your journey to becoming a social worker by completing your three-year degree and are about to embark on what will be a continuing professional developmental pathway throughout your career. It is highly likely that since starting your qualifying course your ideas about what it means to be a social worker have undergone some changes as you have started to become more familiar with what the task involves. We hope that those changes have not diminished your enthusiasm for your chosen career, and later in this chapter we shall examine motivation for choosing social work as a career.

Where are we now?

You are starting out on your career path at a time of transition and change, for the profession as well as for society generally. The social work profession has been under considerable scrutiny and this will be discussed a little later. However, the context of your first year in practice is currently one where the country is facing spending cuts and austerity measures as a result of global recession and political change, and these are likely to hit the poorest and most vulnerable in society hardest, with welfare benefits being reformed and huge cuts to the public sector which will inevitably impact on frontline services.

If you pay any attention to the media you could be forgiven for thinking that almost all social workers work with children and families, and certainly many of the cases which hit the headlines and cause public and political outrage focus on child deaths. High-profile cases including the tragic deaths of vulnerable children like Victoria Climbié and Baby Peter Connelly have led to the spotlight being trained on the profession and on safeguarding children in particular, and subsequent enquiries (Laming 2003, 2009) have made recommendations for change which apply to the social work profession as a whole. The Social Work Task Force was set up by the Labour government in February 2009, with a remit to undertake a comprehensive review of frontline social work practice in England in both adult and children's services, and to make recommendations for improvement and reform of the whole profession, across adult and children's services.

Moira Gibb was appointed chair of the Task Force and stated:

> This is a fantastic opportunity to put social work on a new footing for the long term. The country needs a more confident, more effective and more respected social work profession. (Gibb 2009)

The findings of the Social Work Task Force were published in the November 2009 report *Building a Safe, Confident Future* (SWTF 2009), with 15 core recommendations for action. It would be a good idea for you to read this report, as it has shaped your own professional pathway as you embark on your first year in practice. One of the core recommendations was for a new, supported first year in employment, as discussed in Chapter 2 of this book. In January 2010 the Social

Work Reform Board was set up to implement the recommendations of the Social Work Task Force.

Alongside the changes already mentioned, there is also a transformation taking place in the way services for adults are being provided. Services are being personalised, with an underlying principle of giving people the choice to organise their own support and services. This is a very significant change and will fundamentally alter the social work role, which has, in many areas of provision of services to adults, focused on a care management approach and the rationing and gatekeeping of services. What will this mean for you? Optimistically, what it might mean is a return to a more relationship-based approach to social work with adults, and it is likely that this would be more in line with your original ideas about what it means to be a social worker – working to enable people to take control of their own lives. However, Dickens (2009) highlights the risks that 'personalisation could be used to cut costs and force too much responsibility onto people who are not able to cope' (p.33).

As you can see, social work is in a state of transition and change, and this is something which you need to be prepared for. This is not something new, and if you look back over the relatively short history of the profession it has gone through cycles, often driven by social and political change or reaction to public pressure. In the 1960s there were very familiar concerns about juvenile delinquency, and particularly issues for socially disadvantaged children, as well as meeting the needs of an increasing number of older people, particularly those living alone. At the time local government services were fragmented, with social workers working in a number of departments, including children, welfare (which incorporated services for older people and those with a disability), public health, education and housing. In 1965 the Labour government set up a committee to consider the reorganisation of local authority personal social services in England and Wales. The report prepared by the committee was published in 1968 and came to be known as the Seebohm Report (1968). This led to the creation of unified, community-based, local authority social services departments with social workers working generically with a wide range of service users.

Another example of change was the drive by Conservative governments in the 1980s and early 1990s to contract out and privatise public services. For social work, the introduction of the 1990 NHS and

Community Care Act saw a move towards 'de-institutionalisation' with the closure of residential care homes and long-stay hospitals and the introduction of 'care in the community'. This marked a fundamental change in the social work role, particularly in adult services, where the role moved towards care management and the purchase, rather than the provision, of care (Ferguson and Woodward 2009).

More recently, the inquiry into the death of Victoria Climbié (Laming 2003) made recommendations which led to significant reforms, including the dismantling of local authority social services departments into separate departments for children and adults.

These are just some examples which highlight the fact that part of the social work role is to understand and manage change.

Becoming a professional

A good starting point, when discussing professional identity, is to look at what motivated you in the first place to start your training as a social worker. It is unlikely that this involved sticking a pin in a university prospectus and hoping for the best! Social work gets a very bad press and has been seen at times as a failing profession, and the pay is hardly a motivation, so what was it for you? Consider the following questions:

Box 4.1 Why choose to become a social worker?

- What is a social worker?
- When did I first think about becoming a social worker?
- What motivated me?
- Have my life experiences to date influenced my decision?
- Has my personal value base influenced my career choice?
- Have any of my views changed since completing my initial training?

This exercise is likely to have shown that some synergy between aspects of your personal life, values and beliefs attracted you to social work, which is essentially involved in working with people when they are most vulnerable.

``   I wanted to work in a profession that made a difference and not only make money. (NQSW)

I was hugely motivated to become a social worker due to the degree of poverty in my community and to see what could have been done differently for people in that community. (NQSW) **''**

The following definition of social work was adopted by the International Federation of Social Workers (IFSW) in July 2000:

> The social work profession promotes social change, problem solving in human relationships and the empowerment and liberation of people to enhance well-being. Utilising theories of human behaviour and social systems, social work intervenes at the points where people interact with their environments. Principles of human rights and social justice are fundamental to social work. (IFSW 2000)

The Social Work Task Force was set up at a time (in 2009) when the reputation and public understanding of social work were at an all-time low, and therefore one of its aims was to look at ways to promote a greater understanding of what social workers do. In contrast to the IFSW definition of social work, they offer a simpler definition of social work and the role of social workers:

> **Social Work** helps adults and children to be safe, so that they can cope and take control of their lives again.
>
> **Social Workers** [can] make life better for people in a crisis who are struggling to cope, feel alone and cannot sort out their problems unaided.
>
> (SWTF 2009, p.67)

Take a moment to consider both of these definitions, and in particular what has been omitted from the simpler definition in terms of the values and ethics that underpin the profession. What are the implications of this omission in terms of explaining the complexity of the social work role and defining the profession?

Is social work a profession?

It is important to define what we mean by 'a profession' or 'professional identity' and to put to rest any doubts that might be held about whether or not social work is indeed a profession.

Box 4.2 Exercise: What do we mean by 'a profession'?

- What is your understanding of what constitutes a profession?
- Make a list of professions.
- Make a list of traits or features that you think would identify an occupation as a profession.
- Make a list of the traits or characteristics that you think define social work as a profession.

There has been a great deal of debate in the past about whether social work and other similar occupations such as teaching and nursing are professions, or what is sometimes described as a semi-profession. Traditionally the definition of a profession was based on what was known as 'trait theory' which defines a profession by a set of traits or characteristics, and on the basis of which the status of 'profession' was reserved for specialisms such as medicine and law. An example of such a set of traits might be:

- a basis of systematic theory
- authority recognised by the clientele of the professional group
- broader community sanction and approval of this authority
- a code of ethics regulating relationships of professionals with service users and colleagues.

(Greenwood 1957, p.46)

A more contemporary list of traits might include:

- a high proportion of theoretical knowledge
- a lengthy period of education and training (usually university based)

- peer evaluation of competence

- professional association

- code of conduct

- altruistic service.

Social work has sometimes been seen as a semi-profession because it did not meet all of the characteristics of the traditional 'trait' model (for example, around a recognised and specialist theoretical knowledge base). The traditional professions gained professional identity, power and status through the control and possession of specialist knowledge. However, the professional knowledge base for social work draws on a wide range of disciplines, from psychiatry to sociology, and therefore is not unique to the social work profession. You could argue, to the contrary, that precisely the complexity of the knowledge base forms a key characteristic which defines social work as a profession.

Another issue might be that some of the tasks carried out by social workers can be, and are, carried out by a range of other people. For example, many of the tasks undertaken by mental health social workers can be carried out by mental health nurses. Some care management tasks can be, and are, carried out by unqualified workers.

Greenwood's model (1957, p.46) cites 'broader community sanction and approval of authority' as one of the key traits. This could be seen as problematic for social work, as the public understanding of the role of the social work profession in the UK has been at the very least ambivalent, and at worst extremely hostile. However, increasingly over the past decade there has been a positive move towards the increased professionalisation of social work, and if we take the more contemporary list of traits as a benchmark it could be argued that social work meets most of these criteria. For example, there is a growing, specialist knowledge base which complements knowledge from other disciplines. The initial social work training is now a three-year, university-based degree programme, with a requirement for ongoing training linked to registration. It is a regulated profession with clear codes of professional conduct and it could be seen as an altruistic profession, particularly if we think back to the International Federation's definition of social work (IFSW 2000). However, currently social work is not regulated by the profession itself but by a semi-autonomous government body. This will be discussed in more detail later.

There have been many criticisms of trait theory, including that it is very much modelled on traditional professions of medicine and law, and that 'caring' professions like social work and nursing are predominantly seen as female activities and are therefore afforded less status.

Another important issue to be aware of is that social work is regarded differently in different countries and cultures. In the UK the title of social worker has only been legally protected since 2005. In some countries it is unprotected, and the title of social worker can be used by a range of people who may not be qualified. Social work is, on the other hand, afforded much higher status in some countries than it is in the UK and may carry different statutory powers and responsibilities, or indeed may have no statutory role (Banks 2006).

A final but important point to consider is that the traditional occupations such as law and medicine can be seen to hold a high degree of professional autonomy and power, as historically they were not dependent on the state as an employing institution. This may have changed to some extent during the twentieth century with the introduction of the Welfare State and the National Health Service as well as systems like Legal Aid, but nevertheless, they have a tradition of self-regulation and public respect and are generally seen as autonomous professions.

> Autonomy is regarded as an important dimension of professionalism. (Engel 1970, p.12)

In the United Kingdom, social work is very different to traditional professions as the majority of social workers are employed by the state through local authorities, and they are generally regarded with a degree of suspicion by the public. This could be due in part to a misguided understanding of the degree of professional autonomy that social workers hold. For example, some people believe that social workers can just come and remove your children when they feel like it, or deprive you of your liberty! Some of this suspicion is based on stereotypes, but nevertheless there is no doubt that part of the role of social work is to regulate individuals on behalf of the state rather than to work solely in the interest of the individual, and therefore the extent of social workers' professional autonomy is questionable.

Engel (1970) maintained that bureaucratic organisations limited professional autonomy and that the more bureaucratic the organisation, the less likely that the professional will perceive him- or herself as autonomous. There can be very little doubt that as a social worker you will be employed by a highly bureaucratic organisation with many standardised procedures, whether it is a local authority or health setting. However, it is possible that you will be working within the voluntary sector and therefore may feel that you have a greater degree of autonomy, depending on the culture and structure of the organisation. At this stage in your career you may not be concerned with autonomy as you start to become familiar with your role and are probably glad to have standardised policies and procedures to follow.

Working with other professionals

As a social worker you will inevitably be working with other professions, often within multi-disciplinary teams where the predominant profession will not be social work. Given the discussion above about the nature and status of professions, are there any challenges to inter-professional or partnership working?

> " I work in a multidisciplinary team and feel one of the main challenges in the team is around professional value judgements and what works best for service users. (NQSW) "

Some of the challenges might include different professional values which may lead to conflicting perspectives; professional self-interest, particularly where budgets are involved; different professional boundaries, eligibility criteria, timeframes and poor communication.

Box 4.3 Dealing with challenges to your professional identity

• Think of situations which might lead to conflicting perspectives.
• How would you, as a newly qualified worker, manage this type of situation?

Working in a multi-disciplinary team, particularly as a newly qualified social worker, can be challenging, as you are likely to be less confident in your own professional identity at this early stage and it is human nature to feel intimidated by others who you may think hold more power, either in terms of status or in terms of knowledge, experience and expertise. There are several ways of managing this, which include having a clear idea of your own professional identity and role.

It is very important that you understand the roles of other team members, how the group communicates and how decisions are made. The contributions of all team members should be valued and judgements and prejudices avoided, but this might not be the case. It is important that you are aware of the power dynamics within the multi-disciplinary team and consider who has the most power. You might find that other members of the same team are competing for power, or that within the team certain members have higher status than others. If you are working in this type of team it is important to be aware that there may not be a shared language or common understanding of issues. One of the risks arising from this is that there may be entrenched negative views of other professional groups. Reynolds (2007, p.443) refers to these as 'professional narratives that maintain ritualized ways of working and reinforce professional boundaries'. It is important not to fall into this way of thinking because it perpetuates barriers to successful inter-professional working. If you talk to experienced practitioners it is common for them to acknowledge some of the barriers, but to add that they have formed good relationships with individuals, which can assist good communication.

In terms of your professional identity, what is distinctive about social work is that it considers a person's needs holistically, within the context of their whole life rather than just one aspect of it. Other professionals may only be concerned with a specific area such as health, housing needs or welfare, whereas social work will be looking at the needs of the whole person and how different needs are interconnected. For example, if you work in a hospital setting, a person may be deemed by medical practitioners to be fit for medical discharge – but this does not mean that the appropriate support networks are in place in the community or that their home environment is suitable for them to return to.

Seeing an individual in the context of their family, friends and community, and reflecting their hopes and fears for their own future, is where social work can bring an important contribution to the work of the team. (Department of Health, ADASS *et al.* 2010, p.4)

The social work role is complex, and at any time might involve a number of functions including those of:

- counsellor

- advocate

- partner

- assessor of risk or need

- care manager

- agent of social control.
  (Scottish Executive Education Department 2005)

Your professional identity is underpinned by your professional values and professional knowledge, and it is important to use these as part of the framework that informs your practice in whatever setting you find yourself working. You will be guided by your own agency policy and procedure as well as by legal frameworks. Later we will look at the acquisition of professional knowledge, and part of this process is about 'enculturation' or learning about the culture of your working environment and your place in it.

Professionalism

What do we mean by professionalism? When we say someone has acted in a professional way or done a professional job, what does this mean? Is it linked to the concept of professionalism as we have considered it above, looking at specific traits or characteristics, or does it mean different things in different contexts? When commenting on a job done for us by someone like a builder or gardener, we might say that it was done professionally. In other words it was a job done well to a required standard. However, building or gardening would not traditionally be regarded as professions. What we are perhaps referring to is that the task was performed competently and in line with our expectations and values. Does this apply to social work or do we think of professionalism in a different way (Beckett and Maynard 2005)?

Certainly this understanding of professionalism is pertinent to social work because the way we present ourselves; the way we dress; the way that we communicate with service users and other professionals; timekeeping; doing what we said we would do, when we said we would do it, and other practical issues, as well as skills and competence, are all important to the impression that we create and the way we will be regarded by individuals, other professions and society generally. However, for social work, like other professions, there are clear codes of conduct, values and principles which influence how you carry out your professional role.

As a social worker you are in a position of power, whether this is as a gatekeeper to services or in terms of your statutory powers and responsibilities in certain roles, and therefore awareness of this power is important when working with service users who generally have less power. You need to be able to walk a fine line between being professional and acknowledging the responsibilities that come with your role, and not disempowering those with whom you work. Inevitably there will be occasions where you will exercise your power over an individual as part of your role, but it is important to do so consciously, acknowledging the implications of this for the individual involved. You must also be prepared for times when your professional responsibilities conflict with your professional and personal values – for example, where resourcing issues result in a change of criteria for the allocation of services within your employing agency, leading to you having to withdraw services you previously assessed as a need.

> Behaving 'professionally' in this sense is not just about skill, or competence, or conscientiousness, but something more specific. It is about
>
> a) playing the role that you signed up to when you joined the profession, and
>
> b) setting aside your personal feelings where they conflict with the role.
>
> (Beckett and Maynard 2005, p.73)

Professional knowledge

Think of your first year in practice as an apprenticeship or as a time to build expertise and develop from a novice to a professional with professional knowledge. Boshuizen *et al.* make a distinction between academic knowledge and professional knowledge:

> The relationship between academic knowledge and professional knowledge is important because the former is transformed into the latter through learning in the workplace. (Boshuizen *et al.* 2004, p.5)

You have already had the opportunity through your practice placements to start to translate academic knowledge into professional knowledge, and this first year in practice is the opportunity to build on this in your chosen area of practice.

It is likely that on starting your first job you will be feeling a bit like a fish out of water and as if your qualifying course has not equipped you with the skills that you need for practice. That is not the case, however, as what you have learned so far will provide a foundation on which to start to build your skills and expertise. Some professions like teaching and medicine have a clear pathway of moving from formal education into a more practical phase within a work-based setting like a school or hospital. The introduction of the Newly Qualified Social Worker status emulates this, offering an opportunity to build your specialist knowledge and skills and become familiar with the policy and procedures of your organisation and 'at least as important – [to become] socialised into the culture of the profession' (Boshuizen *et al.* 2004, p.6).

Box 4.4 Developing professional expertise

Boshuizen et al. break down the process of developing expertise into the following domains:

* Learning as the acquisition and improvement of knowledge and skills.
* Learning as a self-directed and self-organised effort to improve performance.
* Learning as the development of a personal identity including emotion management and self-control.
* Learning as enculturation.

Source: Boshuizen *et al.* 2004, p.7

> The continuing development of the sector's workers beyond their induction, initial training and qualifications is an area of crucial importance for social care organisations, their workers and people who use services. (Skills for Care 2010b)

There can be little dispute that ongoing professional development is fundamental to becoming a professional and maintaining standards of practice. If at any point in your career you get to the point where you think that you know it all, you should be very worried! The world that we live in is fast paced and knowledge has to be continuously updated to keep abreast of scientific and technological advances and the ongoing development of theory and research, as well as societal changes. None of us would wish to be treated by a doctor who had not kept up to date with medical advances, and the same can be said for social work. The challenge for the profession is that it draws its knowledge base from such a wide range of disciplines, and it is therefore essential to continuously update and develop your knowledge and experience.

You will find this very challenging, as there is little time on the rollercoaster of practice to spend reading and researching – but nevertheless, this is a professional requirement. There is an expectation that your practice as a professional social worker will be 'evidence-informed', or 'evidence-based' as it is sometimes called. This means that your interventions will be informed by the most current, reliable evidence available and you will integrate this with experience and professional judgement and expertise to come to a decision. There is also a requirement for you to keep up to date with legal frameworks and the policy context of your work. There will be formal opportunities as your career progresses for you to undertake further study, but it is important that you take personal responsibility for the ongoing development of your professional knowledge base.

You have completed the first formal part of your training by undertaking your qualifying degree. You now have the opportunity to build on that knowledge and start to relate it to practice experiences. Applying theory to practice as a student in your academic work can often feel difficult and unnatural. As you become more experienced it should start to make more sense, and you will have more practice experiences on which to base decisions. You will start to see patterns, similarities and differences, which will guide you. You will also become more familiar with policies and procedures, as well as frameworks and tools designed to guide you.

It is important that professional learning is not seen just as a process of acquiring new knowledge, skills and experience. It is also important to understand that part of developing your professional identity and professional learning will be the process of enculturation into your professional group, including the 'acquisition of the skills, habits, attitudes of a certain profession and as a process of becoming accepted and legitimised in a certain context' (Boshuizen *et al.* 2004, p.6). Part of the enculturation process will also be about developing your own personal identity as a social worker and understanding how to transfer knowledge and skills to changing contexts.

> Maintaining a personal identity is of the utmost importance in today's rapidly changing working and social life. In other words, adaptability to continuously changing constraints is a focal element of professional expertise. It is this unstable nature of the environment (i.e. working conditions, task content, and organisational structures) that require stability in the expert's knowledge, skills and attitudes. (Boshuizen *et al.* 2004, p.7)

This is an extremely important point to understand at this stage in your career because, as previously mentioned, social work has always been subject to change but, it could be argued, never more so than at the current time. Generally, social workers who have a strong sense of their own personal identity and confidence in their professional knowledge and expertise cope better with changing contexts.

The role of regulatory bodies

As previously mentioned, over the past decade there has been a gradual professionalisation of social work, beginning in 2001 with the creation of the General Social Care Council, which is the regulatory body for the social work profession in England. (Each country within the UK has its own regulatory council.)

The standards of conduct of traditional professions like law and medicine are largely controlled by members of that profession. An example of this would be the regulatory authority for the medical profession, the General Medical Council, which draws the majority of its membership from the medical profession, for the most part elected by the profession itself. In contrast to this, the General Social Care Council (GSCC) has no members who are elected by the social work profession, and although some do come from the profession, they are all appointed by the government.

The role of the council has been to set the standards for social work education and for social work practice. This includes setting and enforcing codes of practice and maintaining a compulsory professional register of all social workers. Registration has been seen as a way of bringing the social work profession into line with other regulated professions like medicine, nursing and teaching. As a registered social worker, you are currently required to renew your registration every three years with a requirement that you undertake additional training and professional development during this period.

It is important to be aware that in July 2010, the coalition government announced the disbandment of the GSCC. The regulation of social workers is to be the responsibility of the Health Professions Council (HPC). One of the concerns about the disbandment of the GSCC and the incorporation of social work into an organisation which is primarily concerned with medical professions like dieticians, paramedics and physiotherapists, is that the professional identity of social work will be misunderstood and diluted. Moira Gibb (2010), in her role as Chair of the Social Work Reform Board, voiced her concern in a letter to government ministers and stated: 'We hope to ensure that the Health Professions Council (HPC) has a clear understanding of the distinct needs of the social work profession, and is well informed of our work to improve it, ahead of taking on the regulatory roles of the GSCC.'

It is important for you to be aware that one of the recommendations of the Social Work Task Force is that a licence to practise will be introduced, and is expected to take effect in 2016. This will mean that, following graduation, an assessed first year in employment will have to be completed before a licence is awarded. This is likely to be linked to professional development and career structures. It may sound daunting but, as previously stated, it is important as a professional constantly to update your skills and knowledge and to be held accountable for your own professional practice.

The codes of practice set out the standards of professional conduct and practice required of social workers throughout the UK as they carry out their role. All four regulatory councils worked together to develop the codes to contribute to raising standards. They are intended to be a set of clear standards that can be expected of the profession by employers, service users, carers and the public. If there are concerns about misconduct, the GSCC will carry out appropriate enquiries and the outcome of these enquiries will determine whether there is a question about continued registration. You should make sure that you have a copy of the codes of conduct because you are accountable to the public, your employer and the regulatory body for abiding by them. If you are found to be in breach of the codes of conduct, the GSCC conduct committee can impose the following:

- removal from the Social Care Register, which would prevent you from working as a social worker

- suspension from the Social Care Register, which would prevent you from working as a social worker for a set period of time

- admonishment (a mark next to your name on the Social Care Register).

Details of conduct hearings are in the public domain and can currently be accessed on the GSCC website: www.gscc.org.uk. Have a look at these; they will give you an insight into the types of conduct issues that are investigated, and the consequences.

Box 4.5 Exercise: Social work codes of conduct

- What do you understand by the term 'unprofessional conduct'?
- Think of types of behaviour which might be seen to be in breach of the codes of conduct.

There is also a code of practice for employers, which clearly states their responsibility in the regulation of social care workers. It is important for you to be aware of this and of the role that your employer plays in notifying the GSCC about social worker misconduct. This role is currently under review to see if any aspects of this responsibility need to be underpinned by legislation. If you look at some of the details of conduct hearings on the GSCC website you will see that many of these relate to practice issues such as poor or false recording and failure to carry out statutory visits.

Values and ethics in social work

Why is it important to think about values and ethics in social work? Are social work values and ethics fundamental to professional identity? Do values and ethics play the same role in contemporary social work as they have done in the past? What are values?

Parrott (2006) describes social work as:

> a practical-moral activity. This means that social workers hold a privileged position within the public services in working with people who often experience profound problems and significant crises in their lives which require practical solutions but have important moral consequences. (Parrott 2006, p.3)

Throughout your qualifying course, you will have become familiar with all of the National Occupational Standards for Social Work, which clearly identify that social work values are fundamental to the social work role.

> Key role 6: Demonstrate professional competence in social work practice.
>
> • Work within the principles and values underpinning social work practice.
>
> • Identify and assess issues, dilemmas and conflicts that might affect your practice.
>
> • Devise strategies to deal with ethical issues, dilemmas and conflicts.
>
> (Skills for Care 2004, p.17)

The word 'value' has a number of meanings, which include the value of something or what it is worth. One example taken from the *New Oxford English Dictionary*, revised edition (2000) is:

> (Values) A person's principles or standards of behaviour: one's judgements about what is important in life: as in *they internalise their parents' rules and values*... (quoted in Beckett and Maynard 2005, p.6)

Box 4.6 Exercise: Values – personal, societal, professional

What do we mean by the following?

* Personal values
* Societal values
* Professional values

Think of examples of when these different sets of values might conflict.

" Working in a multi-disciplinary team there are often conflicts of opinion, particularly when my health colleagues want somebody discharged from hospital into a residential placement and I feel they should be supported at home because this is what they say they want. (NQSW) "

Personal values

We all have a set of personal values which influence the choices we make, guide our actions and are fundamental to our personal identity. When you thought about your motivation for becoming a social worker, it was suggested that your own personal values might have influenced your decision and that there might be a synergy between your personal values and the broader values and principles highlighted in the International Federation for Social Work's definition of social work. Personal values are influenced by many things, including your own personal experiences and family or cultural influences, or may have a religious or political foundation. There will inevitably be times when your personal values conflict with your professional role and it is crucial to being a professional that you are aware of the potential your personal values have to impact on your professional practice.

Societal values

These are values which are dominant within wider society although they may not have full consensus. Powerful groups in society, particularly religious groups or political parties, are able to impose their values on the rest of society. Societal values can influence personal values but may also conflict with other value systems, such as your culture or religion. As a social worker it is important to be aware of dominant societal values and beliefs because there will be times when your practice and the decisions that you make will conflict with societal values and attitudes – for example, detaining someone under the Mental Health Act and depriving them of their liberty, or removing children from their families, can sometimes be seen as conflicting with widely held values about personal liberty or family life. Paradoxically, if a tragedy occurs as a result of not detaining someone or not removing a child from an abusive situation, society is quick to demonise the social work profession as ineffectual and failing to meet societal expectations of safeguarding individuals or the public. You will frequently hear social workers say, 'We are damned if we do and damned if we don't.' You will have to become used to managing complex ethical dilemmas, as it is fundamental to your professional role.

Professional values

Perhaps a good place to start any discussion is to clarify our understanding of social work values. Where do you find a definitive list? How do we know that we are working in accordance with a set of values? The answer is, it is difficult and complex and there is not a clear set of rules. Shardlow (1998) argues that:

> Getting to grips with social work values is rather like picking up a live, large and very wet fish out of [a] running stream. Even if you think you have caught it, the fish will vigorously slither out of your hands and jump back in the stream. Values and ethics similarly slither through our fingers for a variety of reasons: we don't try hard enough to catch them, preferring the practical business of doing social work. (Shardlow 1998, p.106)

If we look at traditional social work values, you can see that they focus on the individual:

- individualisation

- purposeful expression of feelings

- controlled emotional involvement

- acceptance

- non-judgemental attitude

- client self-determination

- confidentiality

- respect for persons

- congruence

- empathy

- unconditional positive regard.

(Adapted from Biestek 1961)

It is important to understand that social work is a dynamic profession that has been subject to considerable change over the years, often in response to public or political criticism, and this has influenced the development of the professional value base. In the 1960s it was thought that social work was too narrowly focused on the individual and failed to take account of the wider social and political context of people's lives. This led to changes in social work practice and a move towards what was known as 'radical social work' which took into account the impact of structural factors such as inequality and discrimination. This wider and more inclusive focus led to developments in the professional value base and laid the foundations of anti-oppressive and anti-discriminatory practice and what are known as 'emancipatory' values, which built on the more individualistic, traditional values identified above (Thompson 2006). Over the last two decades service user movements have also promoted the importance of putting their needs at the centre of social work practice and service provision, and this has also affected the development of the value base.

/ The principle of *anti-oppressive practice* led to practice values which included:

- empowerment

- partnership

- minimal intervention. /AOP

Working

Anti-discriminatory practice focuses particularly on issues of class, race, age disability, gender, sexuality and language and requires social workers to challenge all forms of discrimination in others and to eliminate it from their own practice (Thompson 2006). *Anti-oppressive practice* has a broader sense and means to endeavour to challenge power differences which are embedded in society (Parrott 2006).

As a newly qualified social worker, recognising discrimination and oppressive practices in others may be relatively straightforward, but you may find it hard to *challenge* it because of lack of confidence. Supervision, formal or informal, is a useful forum in which to seek help and support with this. Do not forget the importance of recognising these issues in your own practice.

As the focus of social work evolved, statements of values have also evolved to include a blend of traditional and emancipatory values. The Central Council for Education and Training in Social Work (CCETSW), which preceded the GSCC as the statutory authority for ensuring standards of social work education and training, laid out the following value requirements, which state that social workers need to:

- identify and question their own values, and their implications for practice

- respect and value uniqueness and diversity, and recognise and build on strengths

- promote people's rights to choice, privacy, confidentiality and protection, while recognising and addressing the complexities of competing rights and demands

- assist people to increase control of and improve the quality of their lives, whilst recognising that control of behaviour will be required at times in order to protect children and adults from harm

- identify, analyse and take action to counter discrimination, racism, disadvantage, inequality and injustice, using strategies appropriate to role and context

- practise in a manner that does not stigmatise or disadvantage individuals, groups or communities.

(CCETSW 1998, p.7)

Because it is impossible to have a definitive, universal list of values which would cover all areas of ethical practice, organisations including the British Association of Social Workers (BASW) and the IFSW have developed codes of ethics which set broader guidance and principles to guide practice.

The introduction of regulation and of codes of practice has in some ways overshadowed social work values and placed more emphasis on what social workers 'must' do in terms of responsibilities for which they are held to account, rather than on a set of values and ethics which 'guide' practice. However, it is likely that in spite of this, adherence to a set of values and ethics based around those identified above by BASW and IFSW will be fundamental to your own professional identity and that of your social work colleagues.

Box 4.7 Social work codes of ethics

BASW – key principles

- human dignity and worth
- social justice
- service to humanity
- integrity
- competence.

IFSW – principles

- human rights and human dignity
- social justice
- professional conduct.

For expanded versions of these, look on the relevant websites:

www.basw.co.uk

www.ifsw.org

...social work often deals with deeply personal and painful issues – mental illness, disability, the personal care of old people, the safety of children – the practice of social work has the potential to challenge deep-seated value positions on many subjects which most people do not even have to think about. (Beckett and Maynard 2005, p.3)

These are the types of complex issues which you will have to learn to deal with as a professional social worker, and you must be aware not only that you have to work within your own professional value base, but also that you may be working with others who have a very different value base. If you talk to experienced practitioners it is likely that they will say that it is their fundamental belief in the principles, values and ethics of the profession that sustains them in working in challenging situations.

Key considerations

- Transition and change are an ongoing feature of the organisation and delivery of social work, and a strong sense of professional identity is important in adapting to and coping with change at an organisational and national level.

- Developments over the past decade, including increasing regulation, introduction of a degree qualification, the requirement for continuing professional development linked to registration and a developing knowledge base, have led to the increasing professionalisation of social work.

- Inter-professional working and multi-disciplinary teams are a feature of social work with adults, and an understanding of your own professional role and identity, as well as those of other professionals, is an important part of working effectively in these settings.

- Developing a professional identity includes the transformation of academic knowledge into professional knowledge through practice experience, as well as the process of enculturation into a team and the development of your personal identity as a social worker.

- Standards of professional conduct and practice are set out in the codes of practice that provide a framework for what social workers 'ought' to do. You are unable to work as a professional social worker unless you are included on the social work register, and any breach of professional conduct will compromise this.

- Professional values and ethics are a fundamental characteristic of social work and your professional identity. The link between your own personal values and the values of the profession was probably a motivating factor in your choice of career and is likely to sustain you through the challenges of your professional life. As the profession has evolved, so has the value base, to reflect the changing nature of society and our understanding of the impact of structural oppression.

Chapter 5

Understanding the Professional Role and Task

- Welcome to the profession
- Defining roles and tasks
- The wider context of practice
- Motivation and meaning

Welcome to the profession

You are entering a profession that is frequently at the centre of political debate surrounding the role of the state in individuals' and families' lives, where even the status of social work as a 'profession' is challenged. Wider society's understanding of the professional social work role and tasks you will engage in is often confused, driven as it is by negative media coverage that frequently misrepresents both social workers and those who access services, and leads to unhelpful perceptions and expectations of you as a social work practitioner. Such misconceptions are not new, and as an activity social work is likely to remain a contentious occupation. However, whilst wider society might not always be clear about what you do, it is important that *you* have a understanding of what will be expected of you as you enter employment.

The completion of your qualifying programme is clearly not only an ending, as discussed in Chapter 1, but, which is more important, a new beginning, as you make the transition from student to professional. The last chapter highlighted the importance of developing your professional identity, and the next step is to integrate your professional identity with your practice. To achieve this you need to engage successfully with the professional roles and tasks expected of a qualified social worker. Many NQSWs experience a period of adjustment at this time, as their expectations of what they will do in the workplace clashes with the reality of practice, especially in statutory settings where bureaucracy, resourcing issues and management systems sometimes appear to take precedence over promoting choice and control for those individuals you work with.

It is important preparation for practice to develop your knowledge of professional roles and tasks and be aware of factors that may influence the way in which you will practise. This will help support you in managing this initial period of adjustment and give you an opportunity to plan ahead. Professional roles and tasks are not static; they are subject to change as society and the politicians who represent the electorate make decisions about the role of social work in individuals' lives. An important aspect of your developmental journey to becoming a confident, competent and capable professional is to ensure that you not only know what tasks they are and how to do them, but also why you are undertaking them.

The first part of this chapter provides guidance on defining the professional role and tasks and then explores factors that will shape them, along with possible tensions that you might encounter in attempting to meet them, once in practice. The second part of the chapter identifies the importance of maintaining your motivation in developing the necessary skills and knowledge to undertake professional roles and tasks.

Defining social work roles and tasks

A logical place to begin is to clarify what we mean by 'roles' and 'tasks' in social work. When discussing the professional role we are referring to the actions and activities assigned to, or required of, the social work profession in general, and you as an individual practitioner. 'The social work task' relates to specific pieces of work required to be done, and purposeful activities that need to be accomplished, within a defined period of time. To understand what these might consist of, you also need to have a clear understanding of the purpose of social work, as this then gives insight into any professional roles or tasks expected of you.

There is no definitive answer to the question 'What do social workers do?' that can be applied to all those who work in the profession. This is because, depending on the service user group you work with and where you work, in terms of geographic location and practice setting, what you do will vary to some extent. However, the General Social Care Council (GSCC), drawing on the International Federation of Social Workers' (IFSW) definition, has developed an 'umbrella' statement that encapsulates the essence of social work and provides clarity about the overarching role and task of social work. This provides a good foundation on which to build as you enter employment:

> The social work profession promotes social change, problem solving in human relationships and the empowerment and liberation of people to enhance well-being. Utilising theories of human behaviour and social systems, social work intervenes at the points where people interact with their environments. Principles of human rights and social justice are fundamental to social work. (GSCC 2008, p.9)

Whilst at a 'macro' or structural level, social workers have this overarching defining role, you will also have to undertake a variety of 'micro' roles and tasks in practice. By 'micro' we mean the day-to-day activities you will actually engage in as a professional. Sometimes the macro and micro levels of practice appear in opposition to one another, and this can become a source of stress as you move through your career, if you lose sight of the overarching role of professional social work. This is where the role of supervision is central to helping explore competing demands and tensions.

For example, you may be asked in the future to undertake an assessment of an individual's mental health to establish whether detention in a psychiatric hospital is necessary. Alternatively, you may also be required to assess that same individual's eligibility for a direct payment or individual budget, whereby they can arrange and manage their service provision in a manner that suits them. The role of the social worker in the first instance is to 'protect'. The tasks that you undertake in order to achieve this might include detaining someone against their will, but in their best interest, so as to minimise any potential harm that could otherwise be caused to themselves or the public. In the alternative scenario, your role is to 'promote choice and control' and the autonomy of the individual. Whilst each role has a different *purpose* at the time of undertaking it at a micro level, both tasks aim to meet the macro role of social work: to empower the individual. Whilst detention in a psychiatric hospital may not at first glance appear empowering, hospital treatment is sometimes required to enable an individual to regain control in their life, and so exercise choice at a later date. Both roles, and the tasks associated with them, should be viewed in the context of the GSCC statement.

Box 5.1 Social work roles and tasks

Re-read the GSCC statement and list the roles and tasks you can identify as encapsulated within it. Ask yourself, what knowledge and skills will you need to use, or develop, to achieve those roles and tasks?

Frameworks such as key roles, occupational standards and professional capabilities provide further guidance on what the professional role is and the tasks you will be expected to perform, along with practical guidance about what support you should expect in your place of work (for example, induction, NQSW provision, CPD strategies, and professional registration requirements (Donnellan and Jack 2010) – see Chapters 2, 3 and 8 for more guidance). These strategies provide an important overview of the professional roles and tasks you might be expected to engage in; however, to develop a more sophisticated understanding of what will be expected of you in practice in adult and mental health settings, it is also necessary to conceptualise social work within a contemporary social and political context and to acknowledge the interrelationship between policy, legislation and social work practice. This is something we keep referring you back to – see Chapters 3 and 4, for example.

Policy, legislation and practice

Health and social care policy and legislation aims to influence, change and shape public behaviour (Dolan *et al.* 2010). It has a similar impact on the professional roles and tasks you will be expected to undertake. Government uses 'hard' instruments such as legislation and regulation to compel you to act in certain ways, whereas 'soft' instruments such as policy and guidance play a less coercive role than legislation, but are coercive in other ways, for example in leading practitioners to follow procedures rather than exercise professional judgement. Policy and legislation provide an important guide to professional practice, and a clear framework within which to work. They also provide security and boundaries that can help you feel safe in the initial stages of your professional life. However, if you just 'do' the job by following policy and legislation alone, you will eventually become demotivated and deskilled as you begin to realise that the circumstances and individuals you work with do not always easily 'fit' into a generic system of practice framed by policy and legislation.

Understanding the social and political context is just as important as understanding the psychological or sociological theories that underpin practice, because ultimately they will shape the form of policy and legislation that you will be expected to use, and will define the purpose of social work and the roles and tasks that you will have to undertake. More often than not, social work is swimming against the tide of social and political change. This is not a bad thing, but continually swimming against the tide is tiring. Policy and legislation can help you understand the government's aims and objectives – and whilst you may or may not agree with those objectives, being aware of them enables you to develop a professional voice to support the people you work with. This is important, because developing an informed, professional opinion can improve your chances of being heard, and can effect change, which is at the heart of social work. Being listened to may also make the difference between your sinking or swimming as a social worker in the longer term!

You will have explored policy, legislation and ideology during your qualifying programme, and you will be aware of the role that policy and legislation have in practice from your placement experiences. Chapter 3 looked at how important it is to use your knowledge base to support you as you prepare for your new role. It is not the purpose of this book to provide critique and analysis of this subject area, therefore you may need to revisit qualifying texts and assignments to refamiliarise yourself with key concepts. At the very least you should have a basic awareness of the changing landscape of practice.

> ❝ On the one hand practice is all about people, and on the other it feels like it's just about resources and form filling, the trick is making sense of how it all interacts to try and ensure that I see the situation from a variety of perspectives, which will mean my practice is not oppressive. (NQSW) ❞

The context of practice in adult and mental health services

The organisation and delivery of adult and mental health social work services across the United Kingdom has seen significant change in the years since 2000. Government has sought to restructure the process of assessment, service development and delivery of health and social care services. Policy from central government has focused on the modernisation of health and social care, with social policy and legislation emphasising service user choice and control along with rights and responsibilities. Central to current practice in adult and mental health services is the development of 'personalised' responses to individual need via the introduction of payments to those eligible for services, which the individual can use to purchase services that they feel will meet their needs. The protection of those who might be at risk of, or vulnerable to, abuse features highly in services for older people and people with learning disabilities, whilst the protection of the public from those who might cause harm is now prevalent in legislation supporting mental health services. For those who may lack mental capacity, protective frameworks provide practitioners with the necessary policy, guidance and legislation to ensure that their practice is anti-oppressive and anti-discriminatory.

Each of these developments has a direct impact on the roles and tasks you will be expected to undertake. Table 5.1 demonstrates the relationship between social work roles and tasks and policy and legislation.

Chapter 3 and Appendix III provide an overview of some policy and legislation that you may need to become familiar with during your induction period. Revisit those key pieces of policy (whether local or national) and legislation, and construct your own table to identify how they shape your social work role and the tasks you have to undertake.

Table 5.1 Policy and legislation and social work roles and tasks

Policy/Legislation	Role	Task
Eligibility Criteria for Adult Social Care (Department of Health 2010b)	Determine eligibility to services	Undertake assessment
No Secrets (Department of Health and Home Office 2000)	Safeguard vulnerable or at-risk adults	Engage in investigation of allegations of adult abuse
Valuing People Now (Department of Health 2009c)	Promote choice and control for those with a learning disability	Personalised assessment, Resource Allocation System (RAS)
Mental Capacity Act 2005	Promote autonomy – assume mental capacity	Undertake assessment
Mental Health Act 1983 (amended 2007)	Statutory protection	Co-ordinate mental health assessment
Community Care (Delayed Discharges, etc.) Act 2003	Ensure timely discharge	Undertake assessment, ensure that discharge not delayed

Daily 'core' tasks

Alongside the roles and tasks expected of you at a macro level you should also consider what tasks you do on a daily basis at a micro level. To fulfil the professional roles and tasks expected of you as a qualified social worker will require a considerable amount of organisation of your time and energy to ensure that you are practising as efficiently and effectively as possible. Donnellan and Jack (2010) identify the variety of tasks involved in social work practice and helpfully suggest monitoring the tasks you perform over a two-week period to enable you first, to reflect on whether the reality of practice is meeting your initial expectations, and second, to use the information gained from this exercise to guide discussion in supervision on any changes that might be required in terms of the type of work you are currently undertaking or areas of development for the future.

Box 5.2 Time spent on core tasks

What tasks take up your time?

Keeping a record of core tasks over a period of, say, two weeks will help you to see more broadly how you are spending your time.

		Working with service users/carers	Working with families	Working with groups and communities	Preparing reports for boards, panels, court	Assessment and support planning	Data entry; information management systems	Admin: correspondence/email	Liaising with other professionals	Liaising within team or agency	Supervision	Training/CPD activities	Allocation: meetings/discussion	Accessing research; internet and intranet and reflect on practice	Travel
WEEK 1	Mon														
	Tues														
	Wed														
	Thurs														
	Fri														
WEEK 2	Mon														
	Tues														
	Wed														
	Thurs														
	Fri														

Key: Significant time ✓✓   Little time ✓   No time ✗

Source: adapted from Donnellan and Jack 2010

Maintaining motivation

As can be seen from Table 5.1 and Box 5.2, the roles and tasks you will be expected to undertake will be diverse. Professional practice can be exciting and challenging, but fraught with tension and complexity. Look back at the GSCC's overarching statement of the social worker's professional role and tasks (see page 90) and we can see clearly that as a career social work has much to offer; yet research suggests that many social workers lose their initial enthusiasm as the reality of working with individuals who are experiencing difficulty in their lives on a day-to-day basis saps their energy.

It is clear that the main cause of demotivation is not the individuals that social workers work with, but rather the systems that social workers are expected to work in. Jones' (2001) research with social workers employed in the statutory sector suggests that practitioners' biggest source of stress and dissatisfaction comes not from working with service users, but from working within local and national policy guidelines that have been developed in light of inadequate budgets rather than in an attempt to redress inequalities. This has had a profound effect on the profession, as social work practitioners who work with adults are increasingly troubled by the way practice is dominated by concerns about budgets, rather than adhering to social work values or promoting social justice (Galpin 2009).

Horner and Jones' (2004) analysis of public sector recruitment and retention found three key factors that influenced practitioners to join and/or stay in the public sector: making a difference, job satisfaction, and reward packages. More generally, research has shown that social care professionals do have a high intrinsic level of job satisfaction (Cameron 2003) and are motivated by being in meaningful contact with service users (Huxley *et al.* 2005).

Horner and Jones found that 'push' factors, such as feelings of frustration, outweighed 'pull' factors, such as better money, in determining whether social workers stayed in or left the public sector. Despite changes in terms of education and registration and the increased 'professionalism' of social work, some practitioners still feel increasingly estranged from their employers, alienated, burnt out and powerless when it comes to decision making (Jones 2001).

The Social Work Reform Board (SWRB 2010) is clear in its belief that good social work can transform the lives of those you come into contact with, and suggests that social workers need 'stamina, emotional resilience and determination' (p.23) – therefore, keeping motivated is going to be crucial for you in the longer term. The need for a coherent strategy from the outset of your career in social work cannot be emphasised enough, as evidence from a range of industries suggests that structured career development opportunities and pathways are both critical for creating a motivated and stable workforce (Parker and Whitfield 2006).

Until now you will have concentrated your efforts on meeting the requirements of your formal training to develop theoretical knowledge and listening, communication and written skills to support you in undertaking social work roles and tasks; now you will also need to maintain your determination and emotional resilience in order to continue in your development. This will require sustained motivation on your part.

What is motivation?

'Motivation' refers to the drive you direct at meeting or achieving a specific goal, which in this case is to undertake the roles and tasks expected of you professionally and to continue in your development as a capable, competent and confident practitioner in your chosen specialist area. Your motivation will be dependent on extrinsic and intrinsic factors. *Extrinsic factors* are those external incentives or pressures that motivate you into some form of action – for example, professional requirements (like registration), punishments (like a conduct hearing), and rewards (like promotion). When internalised, these motivate change. *Intrinsic factors* are those inner pressures that create a desire to engage in change – for example, values and beliefs.

The limited research available on the motivation of individuals who choose social work as a career suggests that their motivation comes from wanting to help others help themselves and to find answers to problems in wider society, in terms of issues such as equality and justice (Pearson 1973) rather than a quest for power, status and money (Donnellan and Jack 2010). The statement from the NQSW below seems to support this.

I was hugely motivated to become a social worker due to the degree of poverty among people in my community and to see what could have been done differently... I work in a multidisciplinary team and feel that one of the main challenges in the team was around professional value judgments in terms of what works best for service users. (NQSW) **"**

Developing your motivation

Much of the literature around motivation comes from management studies (McGregor 1960; Herzberg 1972) and theories around how adults learn (McClelland *et al.* 1953; Rogers 1993). However, it' is equally applicable to you at this particular time and can offer some useful hints on the factors that can make a difference as you continue to learn and develop as a social worker.

Table 5.2 Meeting Maslow's hierarchy of needs

Maslow's motivational need	Practice: how will this need be met?
Physiological – e.g. water, food, sleep	Lunch/coffee breaks; limited working hours (i.e. 8-hour day); adequate sleep; diet; leisure time; holidays; wages to buy life essentials.
Safety – e.g. security	Secure working environment; job security; induction programme; supervisory arrangements in place.
Social – e.g. belonging, acceptance	Being part of a team – attending team events; membership of a professional body; support networks (family/friends).
Esteem – e.g. self-respect, status	Societal recognition of profession; job title protected by professional registration; positive feedback from employer.
Self-actualisation – e.g. professional growth, advancement	Acheivement in work; challenging work (proportionate growth in level of case complexity); advancement in organisation.

The most well known motivational model is Maslow's (1943) hierarchy of need, which outlines the requirements individuals need in order to reach their full potential and suggests that lower needs should be met before higher needs can be satisfied. The hierarchy of needs (reading upwards) is for *physiological needs, safety, social, esteem* and *self-actualisation*, and is usually represented in the form of a pyramid, with physiological need at the base and self-actualisation at the apex. Once a need is satisfied it ceases to motivate, and the need at the next level above becomes the motivator. So how might this help you in developing your motivation? First, it provides a basic understanding of what types of factors are going to help you in your transition from student to professional. Second, it provides a framework you can use to understand what needs to happen next to help you successfully make the transition from student to professional. Table 5.2 provides an example of how you might use this model.

Motivation and meaning

In all likelihood your motivation has been linked to both intrinsic and extrinsic drivers at different times, and in different circumstances; however, ultimately motivation that is enduring comes from within. That is not to say it is entirely up to you – your employer should also have a role in motivating you in terms of pay, progression and opportunities for continuing professional development; however, whilst such strategies are helpful, research suggests that these have a time-limited effect and that 'meaning' is of equal importance (Huxley *et al.* 2005). Meaning, in this sense, is about those internal drivers; most people who lack meaning in their professional lives lack clarity about their purpose and/or their specific role, and then lose sight of what they are trying to achieve and why.

What do you want from a career in social work; money, prestige, creativity, a sense of pride, security, or happiness...? In order to create meaning in your career, you must decide what makes it meaningful for you.

Research with students suggests that developing your identity along with a sense of purpose is central to the development of meaning. A sense of purpose, in particular, was found 'to be important to the overall development and growth of college students' (Molasso 2006). Chickering and Reisser (1993) identified a number of influences that contribute to developing a positive identity and sense of purpose, or meaning. These include, for example: achieving competence, managing your emotions, developing mature professional interpersonal relationships and developing your professional integrity. These are worth considering as you embark on your journey into the professional roles and tasks of social work.

Box 5.3 Five influences on developing meaning

Think about how these might be achieved and what areas need development, what needs to happen next?

1. Developing competence.

2. Controlling emotions.

3. Moving from professional independence to partnership working.

4. Developing your professional identity.

5. Creating meaning/purpose in your professional role.

Source: adapted from Molasso 2006

Health warning!

Meaning can often be facilitated by allowing individuals to undertake new roles that may carry a higher level of responsibility and/or complexity. Rising to new challenges can add extra meaning to your role and the tasks you undertake. However, be aware that there is a difference between role *enlargement* and role *enhancement*. The former may increase stress levels, whereas the latter may increase motivation, competence and confidence. Improving the meaningfulness of a task is what has the motivational impact – not simply increasing the amount of pressure or volume of tasks!

The potential to make a positive difference to individuals' lives is achievable. However, this will require a clear awareness, on your part, of your professional identity and the skills and knowledge that you will be required to develop to facilitate the transition from student to professional (these were discussed in Chapters 1 and 4). It requires more than taking on ever more complex casework and a high caseload; in the longer term these alone will demotivate you. The greatest role your employer can play in motivating you is to recognise you for who you are and help find a way forward by making the best use of your strengths and abilities. However, your experiences will probably not all be ideal, there will be good points and bad, and the skill is to ensure that the good outweighs the bad. To achieve this you need to put in place a coping strategy to try and facilitate a positive experience.

Stalker *et al.* (2007) suggest that individuals in the caring professions who take an active and engaged approach to coping are more likely to maintain their intrinsic levels of motivation, even when under pressure (Donnellan and Jack 2010) whereas those who take a disengaged approach experience a negative effect. Clearly, being engaged is the best way forward – so how does one become engaged, and what does disengagement look like? Table 5.3 provides some examples of engaged and disengaged behaviour. Which have you used in the past, and did they help or hinder your progress?

Table 5.3 Engaged and disengaged behaviours

Engaged	Disenagaged
Problem solving – raises issues.	Problem avoidance – goes off sick.
Seeking support – communicates with manager and peers; uses supervision to discuss issues/ problems.	Social withdrawal – avoids discussion with others and in supervision; focuses on the pragmatic aspects of practice in supervision.
Expressing emotions – voices concerns, fears.	Self-criticism, wishful thinking – hopes problems and fears will resolve themselves; locates problems and answers within oneself; does not take action.

Key considerations

- It is important preparation for practice to develop your knowledge of professional roles and tasks and be aware of factors that influence the way in which you will meet them.

- Professional roles and tasks are not static; they are subject to change as society and the politicians who represent the electorate make decisions about the role of social work in individuals' lives.

- 'The professional role' refers to the actions and activities assigned to, or required of, the social work profession in general, and you as an individual practitioner.

- 'The social work task' refers to specific pieces of work required to be done and purposeful activities that need to be accomplished within a defined period of time.

- Understanding the social and political context is just as important as understanding the psychological or sociological theories that underpin practice, because they ultimately shape the form of policy and legislation that you will be expected to use, and will define the purpose of social work and the roles and tasks that you will have to undertake.

- Until now you will have concentrated your efforts on meeting the requirements of your formal training to develop theoretical knowledge and listening, and communication and written skills to support you in undertaking social work roles and tasks. Now you will also need to maintain your determination and emotional resilience to continue in your development. This will require sustained motivation on your part.

Part III

Finding the Way Forward

Part III focuses on the time after transition, when your workload is increasing and you begin to experience some of the both positive and stressful aspects of professional practice. Chapter 6 explores the central role of supervision in supporting you in practice, identifying the different types of supervision and the role each has to play in developing good practice, and emphasising your active engagement in the process. The following chapter provides an overview of managing the stress you might experience as a social work professional. Of course, not all stress is negative; stress can act as a motivator. However, in the longer term, to maintain your energy for the profession you will need to develop your understanding of how the job might impact on you and your ability to practise to ensure stress does not develop into 'burnout'. The final chapter leads you to begin thinking about the future, drawing on reflections from your first year in practice to make and develop plans for your future professional development. Remember, gaining your social work qualification was just the start of your journey; much more lies ahead and you just need to work out which way to go to move you forward!

Chapter 6

Taking Part in Supervision

- ❖ The purpose and functions of supervision
- ❖ How to get the most out of supervision – using formal and informal methods
- ❖ Developing a positive working relationship with your supervisor
- ❖ Managing tension within supervision
- ❖ Becoming a supervisor

The current NQSW frameworks for England, Wales, Scotland and Northern Ireland all identify *appropriate supervision* as a key component in ensuring the development and support needs of NQSWs. The frameworks emphasise that regular supervision is crucial in assisting an NQSW to make the transition from being a student to becoming a professional social worker who is effective in their job. It is widely recognised within the literature that supervision is central to social work and social care practice, regardless of the stage you are at in your career (Brown and Bourne 1996; Davys and Beddoe 2010; Hawkins and Shohet 2006; Kadushin 1992; Morrison 2001). 'Skilled supervision strengthens social work practice and ensures robust decision-making' (Field 2008, p.11).

The Social Work Task Force (SWTF) in England reviewed social work practice, recognised that many social workers were not getting high quality supervision, and made recommendations for national requirements underpinning the quantity and quality of supervision (SWTF 2009). You may be reading this chapter as an NQSW entering into a supervisory relationship at the start of your social work career; however, supervision could also support you as a supervisor or manager of qualified staff, as a placement work tutor, or as a student on placement. Supervision is a central part of improving and developing practice, regardless of the stage of supervision or career.

The purpose and functions of supervision

As a starting point it is important to reflect on your own views and expectations around supervision, as these could impact on how you engage with the process, and indeed could prevent you from getting the most out of supervision. Previous experiences of supervision can affect your opinion around whether you feel supervision is useful and can influence your next supervisory relationship; for example, your experience of supervision as a student and the relationship you had with your practice teacher can impact on how you engage with supervision in your first post as a social worker. Therefore, being open and honest about your past experiences of supervision and how you value supervision could prove to be an important starting point in your new supervisory relationship and help you and your new supervisor build a positive and professional relationship.

Box 6.1 Exercise: Why do I need supervision?

Answer the questions below and take them with you to your initial supervision session.

- Think of as many benefits as possible of receiving supervision.
- Think of as many as possible consequences of not receiving supervision, or of receiving poor supervision?
- Have you had a good experience of supervision to date? If yes, try to identify the factors that were important to you in past supervision. If no, try to identify the key issues and tensions from previous supervision.

Sharing this with your new supervisor can help you both to think about the best way to approach supervision and what has worked well (or not so well) in the past.

Much of the literature around supervision identifies the key functions or tasks of supervision as fitting into the following terms: administration or management; teaching or education; and supportive or personal (see Kadushin 1976; Pettes 1967). Inskipp and Proctor (1993) call the tasks of supervision the *normative* task, the *formative* task and the *restorative* task, and other work reflects on alternative functions, including a meditative function (Morrison 2001); a function in developing a strong professional identity (Tsui 2005); and more recently, a method of surveillance of practitioners with a goal to eliminate risk (Peach and Horner 2007). Oko (2009) recognises the importance of the organisational context and places supervision as the mediator between the worker and the tasks of the organisation.

We have already reflected on your own views around the value of supervision, and it is now vital to reflect upon the function and purpose of supervision for employers, in order to gain an understanding of how they intend supervision to be used and how this fits with your own expectations around supervision.

Box 6.2 What provision for supervision is in place in my agency?

- Does your agency have a clear supervision policy and supervision standards?

- Is there a clear definition of supervision that identifies its function and purpose?

It is important to find out about these when starting a new job, and before you meet with your new supervisor, as this may impact on how supervision is organised.

Hughes and Pengelly (1997) provide a useful 'triangle of supervisory functions' which can be used to reflect on the different tensions within the supervision process and competing needs. The three functions identified by Hughes and Pengelly fit with the three interrelated functions recognised within NQSW frameworks – all these are shown in Figure 6.1.

The scenario below demonstrates how important each element of this triangle is for you within an adult setting, and how a balance is required to cover all of the necessary areas.

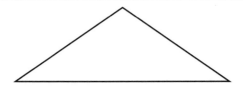

Managing service delivery:
Ensure agency policies, procedures and protocols are followed. Address quality and quantity of work (Hughes and Pengelly 1997).
Line management:
Accountability for practice and quality of service, including managing resources, delegation of work, workload management, performance appraisal (Skills for Care 2009).

Facilitating practitioner's continuing professional development:
Ongoing professional development (Hughes and Pengelly 1997).
Continuing professional development to ensure that the worker has the relevant skills, knowledge, understanding and attributes to do the job and progress in their career (Skills for Care 2009).

Focusing on the practitioner's work:
Reflect upon and explore practitioner's work with clients (Hughes and Pengelly 1997).
Professional or case supervision:
To enable and support practice – review and reflect on practice issues and maximum opportunities for wider learning (Skills for Care 2009).

Figure 6.1 Triangle of supervisory functions
Source: adapted from Hughes and Pengelly 1997

Scenario 1: Laura's supervision needs

Laura is an NQSW who has just started a new job in an older persons' Community Mental Health Team (CMHT). Laura completed a previous student placement within an older persons' social work team and one placement within an adult CMHT, but she has no previous experience of a CMHT for older people. Laura needs her supervision to combine the following three elements:

1. *Managing service delivery/line management*: Laura needs regular supervision to ensure that she has a clear understanding of the team's working policies and procedures and that she is applying these appropriately to her practice. She needs line management of her workload, and management in terms of quality assurance of her practice. She needs close supervision to ensure that any work allocated is relevant in terms of the level of complexity for an NQSW. She also needs her progress monitored in terms of

the outcome statements as an NQSW. She needs opportunities to develop her understanding of the specialist client group she is working with, whilst also reflecting on her core social work skills, knowledge and values.

2. *Professional/case supervision*: Laura needs regular opportunities to reflect on her practice and evaluate her role and decision-making. She needs an opportunity to explore alternative ways of working and identify where maybe things did not go as well as they could have. She needs opportunities to analyse the relevant theoretical approaches that inform her work and reflect on new research evidence that can inform her practice.

3. *Continuing professional development*: Laura's supervision needs to include identification of areas of knowledge and skill that need to be developed, with clear plans around how this can be achieved. Supervision needs to ensure that learning and development time is protected and the right opportunities are available to support Laura's development (e.g. opportunities for shadowing/joint working with more experienced practitioners, additional training, supplementary activities, joining relevant forums, attending conferences). CPD planning and review is an important part of this process.

The impact of supervision on practice

Regardless of what you see as the primary function and whose needs are being met through supervision, the service user and patient features as key participants throughout the process (Hughes and Pengelly 1997), whether you are reviewing your caseload, reflecting on specific issues with an individual service user, reviewing agency policy and procedures which link to the provision of services, or reflecting on your own future learning and development needs as a practitioner to improve knowledge, skills and values in practice with service users. Yelloly and Henkel (1995) link supervision and practice outcomes through the idea of the 'reflective practitioner' – one who is able both to reflect with the service user on their experience, and to encourage change by reflecting on their own practice, for which supervision plays a central part. Therefore effective supervision that supports the practitioner with their tasks in practice and assists them to reflect on their role and actions can have a direct impact on outcomes for service users.

Davys and Beddoe (2010) highlight the reflective learning model for supervision, where supervision is a learning process driven by the experiences of the learner (supervisee) and not the experience and knowledge of the supervisor. This model consists of a four-stage cycle of supervision, leading you from the *event* itself, via *exploration* and *experimentation* to *evaluation*. The stages allow an event or experience from practice to be explored with the purpose of arriving at a new understanding and possible action that is applied back into future practice. This links back to the work of Kolb (1984) (experiential learning model) and Schön (1987) (reflection on action). Kolb's model starts with a person's concrete experience and takes the learner through a cycle of reflection and abstract conceptualisation (analysis), to active experimentation and back to further experience. Davys and Beddoe (2010) recognise that these models of reflection and evaluation of a situation or an experience lead to greater understandings and knowledge of practice, that can be applied back into practice, and that the reflective process within supervision can 'therefore be considered as a transportable learning process which can be internalised and accessed at the worker–client interface' (p.92), leading to greater reflection in action (Schon 1987).

Hawkins and Shohet (2006) consider that there are a number of stages of development for a supervisee and that the stage of development will affect both your needs as a supervisee and the response required of the supervisor. They identify the four stages of development as:

1. *Self-centred childhood*: dependent on supervision, with more doubt around professional judgements and with a need for more teaching within supervision, encouragement and regular feedback.

2. *User-focused adolescent*: moving towards confidence and complexity in judgements but with a need for ongoing reflection.

3. *Process-centred adult*: increased confidence, reflecting on learning, with a need for more challenging supervision.

4. *Process-in-context-centred mature*: moving towards the supervision/ teaching of others, where there is a need to be given more responsibility.

In terms of considering your expectations of supervision, it is important to reflect on the stage that you are at and how this may affect your supervision needs – for example, as an NQSW do you fit into the 'self-centred childhood' category? Or do you feel that your previous experiences place you more within the 'user-focused adolescent' category? These may be important considerations, as your supervisor is also likely to be considering your stage of professional development and your needs, so it can be useful to discuss them openly.

Promoting reflective practice within supervision, and stages of development, will be discussed a little later in the chapter when we look at supervision styles and developing a positive working relationship with your supervisor.

How to make the most of supervision

"   Supervision is so important. My advice? TALK! (NQSW)   **"**

This section of the chapter will discuss *ad hoc*, informal methods of supervision and briefly consider the place of group supervision. Initially we will concentrate on formal, individual supervision.

The NQSW framework for England (Skills for Care 2009) suggests that all NQSWs should be offered formal, one-to-one supervision on at least a fortnightly basis for the first six months in post, and weekly for the first six weeks. Regardless of where you are practising in the UK we would suggest that this is a good framework from which to negotiate supervisory arrangements. The framework also suggests that supervision should address:

- your professional practice – monitoring progress, reviewing and reflecting on practice issues and planning ongoing CPD

- the quality of your work in the organisation and compliance with its policies and procedures.

As discussed already, the starting point for effective individual supervision is confirming the purpose and function from the standpoint of the agency, you as the supervisee, and your supervisor. It may be useful for you and your supervisor to complete the exercise in Box 6.3.

Box 6.3 Exercise: Expectations of supervision

Respond to the following points and ask your supervisor to do the same. Then use within your first supervision session to discuss the function/purpose and tasks of supervision.

I am expecting supervision to focus on/explore the following areas:

- Quality of my work.
- Review of my workload.
- Agency policies and procedures.
- My training and development needs.
- The legislative and policy context that informs my practice.
- The theoretical framework that informs my practice.
- My value base and impact on my work.
- My interaction with colleagues and other agencies.
- To help me consider the emotional impact of practice.
- To monitor my overall health and emotional functioning.
- To help me reflect on any difficulties in relationships with colleagues and to support me in resolving conflict.
- Allocation of resources.
- Other budgetary issues.
- Team responsibilities and roles.
- Organisational developments or information.
- Elements of my personal life impacting on my work and role.

Reflect on any differences in your responses and consider in line with any agency policy on supervision.

Consider what is negotiable and what is not negotiable in terms of what can be offered within your supervision.

Supervision agreements and contracts

There is general agreement that a clear supervision contract or written agreement underpins good supervision. A contract identifies the structure, organisation and arrangements of supervision, identifies roles and responsibilities, considers the content of sessions and expectations, and provides a basis for reviewing the supervisory relationship. Some agencies may have a set contract which you will be expected to work to; therefore it is important for you to check whether there is a contract which you will be expected to sign, or whether you can contribute to setting up a contract with your supervisor.

Box 6.4 Checklist for supervision contract

You may wish to include the following points within your contract. If you are working to a set agency contract, it may be beneficial to check if the contract covers the following areas, and if not, discuss with your supervisor:

- aims of supervision/purpose/expectations from agency and workers
- frequency, duration and location of sessions
- confidentiality issues – to include any limitations on confidentiality
- record keeping – to include who makes records, storage of records and purpose for which records may be used
- agenda setting – to include who sets agenda? When is agenda set?
- preparation for supervision sessions – expectations of all participants
- content and structure of individual sessions, e.g. main work items, case review, specific practice issues, development and training issues, information briefing
- feedback and review of progress
- process for dealing with any difficulties
- missed sessions
- the relationship of supervision to appraisal
- renewal/review of supervision contract.

Although a contract will formalise the supervisory process, this does not guarantee 'purposeful engagement by either or both parties in supervision'. (Morrison 2005, p.118)

Engagement within the supervision process relies on commitment and shared understanding. (This links to the earlier discussion around your previous experiences of supervision and how these may impact on how you engage with new supervision arrangements.) Also, commitment to regular sessions despite having a very busy workload is vital, and at all costs this will mean avoiding having to cancel sessions. Commitment to sessions includes ensuring that you are adequately prepared for supervision, with a clear agenda and some thought as to what agenda items should be prioritised at each session. Showing commitment to supervision will not only mean that your supervisor is more likely to remain committed, come prepared and be less likely to cancel, but will also assist you in getting the most out of the supervisory process. It may be helpful to pencil in future supervision sessions well in advance with your supervisor, so that regardless of how busy either of you gets, your supervision time is already protected.

The more you put into your supervision, the more you are likely to get out of it. (Donnellan and Jack 2010, p.161)

Box 6.5 Preparation for supervision

It may be useful to reflect on the following areas before supervision to help you prepare for a session and put together an agenda.

- Any service user/client contact since the last supervision session that is causing me concern?
- Has my approach/method of working with any service user changed since the last supervision session?
- Have any of my goals/what I am hoping to achieve with any particular service used changed since the last session?
- Do I feel 'stuck' or unable to move forward or unable to identify an achievable goal with any of my service users?
- What pieces of practice/areas of my work do I feel have been going well since my last supervision?

It is important to recognise that a lot will happen to you within the week, fortnight, or even month (depending on the frequency of supervision) between supervision sessions, and equally important to take time to reflect and consider what should be discussed, in advance of the next supervision session. This can't and shouldn't be done five minutes before a session. It may be helpful to pencil into your diary a set time the day before your session, to reflect on what has happened and what you would like to take to supervision. Going back through your diary, where you will have a record of all your recent service user visits and appointments, may help you remember what you have done. Some people find it useful to keep a journal or reflective log of significant events and issues as they occur, to help them prepare for supervision.

It is also worthwhile giving some thought to where supervision should take place. Although it may be practical in terms of travelling time and distance, it may not be the best option to have supervision at your own or your supervisor's work base, as there you are more likely to be interrupted or affected by things going on around you.

It is really important for you to give some thought to supervision records and check out whether there is an agreed method for recording supervision. It is also important to discuss with your supervisor who will take responsibility for record-keeping – for example, is this shared? The following areas may be discussed within supervision and therefore will need to be recorded in an appropriate format:

- case material, client issues, clinical decisions – it is important to record where a supervisor has impacted on decisions about case management (Morrison 2005)

- learning objectives and training issues

- any issues shared by the supervisor (e.g. policy, protocols, organisational procedures)

- any personal issues related to work

- any feedback on performance from the supervisor

- any action points for the supervisee and/or supervisor

- date and arrangements for the next session, including any issues that you need to take forward to the next session.

Informal and ad hoc supervision

It is important to see supervision as much more than planned, formal, one-to-one sessions, and to recognise that unplanned and *ad hoc* supervision with your supervisor should be understood as a normal part of the supervisory relationship (Skills for Care 2009). Supervision can therefore take place in many different settings and can involve many different people. It is important to discuss with your supervisor how *ad hoc*, unplanned situations that necessitate some form of supervision will be handled – for example, a need to urgently follow up on a case discussion that occurred in supervision but where the situation has changed suddenly. It is important to agree how such discussions and outcomes from *ad hoc* supervision are recorded and followed up in a later, formal supervision session.

As an NQSW it is also important to think about how you will use your colleagues and peers to support you. This type of informal supervision from colleagues and peers often takes place within the office environment, in team meetings and peer group forums, and can be extremely valuable in assisting you to reflect on practice decisions and issues, gain feedback from others and discuss alternative approaches which may impact on how you do things in a similar situation on another occasion (see Scenario 2 below). This can be especially valuable within multi-disciplinary teams where a range of professionals from different backgrounds are working together from the same office – *ad hoc*, informal supervision with professionals from different backgrounds allows you to develop a better understanding of your colleagues' different roles and responsibilities, learn from others' expertise and reflect on different working practices.

> **"** The Safeguarding Adults forum makes such a difference, just listening to others talk about their practice has helped me to understand the role and gives me that chance to check out my practice. (NQSW) **"**

Organising professionals into multi-disciplinary teams is now widely accepted practice within many adult services (e.g. mental health, learning disabilities, hospital settings) as multi-disciplinary teams are seen as the most effective way of bringing together the skills, experiences and knowledge of a range of different professionals to meet service users' needs. For example, community mental health teams, assertive outreach teams, crisis intervention and home treatment teams are the main forms of service delivery in adult mental health, and these are usually multi-disciplinary, consisting of nurses, social workers, occupational therapists, clinical psychologists and psychiatrists. The rationale of this set-up is to give access to health and social care services in a coordinated manner, allowing increased contact among those providing care, increased joint working opportunities, joint decision making and mutual support (Ryan and Pritchard 2004). Therefore, ongoing informal supervision among colleagues and the sharing of good practice examples, dilemmas and conflicts can be an essential part of worker development and learning, whilst also creating group support.

Professional forums and groups that are set up to discuss practice situations can be another good means to informal supervision from colleagues: practice examples are shared as a way of contributing to the learning of others, and this can be seen as a form of 'group supervision'. Group supervision, when properly set up and facilitated, can be a useful way of providing all or additional supervision arrangements (Brown and Bourne 1996: Morrison 2005). Group supervision can offer team and/or peer support, a wider pool of skills and knowledge, opportunities for peer modelling and a sense of team cohesion, and can allow greater transparency of practice and reduce over-dependence on a single supervisor (Morrison 2005).

Inter-professional supervision

Within adult services, where policy initiatives have led to the development of many integrated health and social care teams, joint budgets and single line management have now become commonplace, with more examples of inter-professional supervision. For example, an NQSW within a community mental health team may be supervised by a senior practitioner or line manager who is a community psychiatric nurse.

Davys and Beddoe (2010) recognise that a supervisor from another profession may introduce a new range of skills and experiences and raise new challenges to practice. Cassedy *et al.* (2001) agree that it is not the shared professional base that is important, so much as the competence of the supervisor. However, concerns can also be raised that supervision from a person outside of your own profession can contribute to a loss of professional identity. It is important for you to clarify the arrangements for supervision within such settings – for example, is there a difference between *line management* and *professional* supervision (i.e. are you also being offered supervision from a senior member of your own profession)? If you are being offered supervision from two different people, is everyone involved clear about roles and responsibilities? Are supervision notes shared with both supervisors? Are timings between supervisions clear? Are there any plans for occasional joint supervision with both supervisors together?

If there is an expectation that you will be supervised by your line manager from a different professional background and there are no arrangements for professional supervision, it may be useful for you to discuss your views on this with your supervisor and raise issues of professional identity. It will also be useful for you to look into any other means of professional support that may be on offer (e.g. professional networks and/or groups), or possibly in future you could be involved in setting it up yourself.

Scenario 2: Jim's supervision arrangements

Jim is an NQSW who has been in his post at the learning disabilities team for the past six weeks. Jim is receiving fortnightly supervision from his line manager, who is a nurse. It has been arranged that Jim will also receive monthly supervision from a senior practitioner who is a social worker (she is based with the learning disabilities team only for two days a week).

In addition to the arrangements above, Jim is using informal/*ad hoc* supervision with his colleagues. He works in an open-plan office with a mix of nursing colleagues, a social worker, an occupational therapist and a clinical psychologist. They discuss cases and practice issues on a daily basis, and Jim feels comfortable reflecting on his practice with this group of colleagues. There is also a weekly team meeting where all the team members meet to discuss referrals and allocation of work. This meeting also provides an opportunity to discuss any case issues. The clinical psychologist within the team also runs a group supervision session every six weeks with another team, which Jim is planning to attend.

Jim is receiving a good mix of formal and informal supervision, both on an individual basis and with colleagues. This balance between formal and informal methods integrates all of Jim's supervision needs – line management, professional/case supervision and continuing professional development.

Developing a positive working relationship with your supervisor

Learning styles

Supervision is not just about case management: it is also about acquiring and developing new skills and knowledge. Therefore, in order to develop a positive working relationship with your supervisor, there is a need to consider your own learning style and that of your supervisor to find the best ways for you to work together.

We have already looked at how past experiences, expectations, commitment, preparation and the stage of your development can impact upon supervisory approaches and the very effectiveness of supervision; however, individual preferred learning styles need to be acknowledged too (Morrison 2005).

Honey and Mumford (1986) identify four learning styles:

- *Activists* learn best by doing.

- *Reflectors* learn best from reflection, observation and listening.

- *Theorists* learn from analysis.

- *Pragmatists* learn from experimentation.

Acknowledging your own learning style can help you and your supervisor to find an approach that works, recognising your strengths and weaknesses. Morrison (2005) recognises that there are potentially positive and negative outcomes of supervisors and supervisees having shared or similar and different or conflicting styles. For example, 'similar styles' may mean that you do not always consider alternative approaches or courses of action, whereas conflicting styles between the supervisor and supervisee may result in the supervisee frequently feeling challenged and that their chosen approach is 'wrong'. Therefore, having a discussion with your supervisor about your individual learning style can be an important starting point in your supervisory relationship.

Linked to your learning style is the 'learning cycle' that was discussed on page 110 (Kolb 1984). Kolb's cycle is based on the view that there is a process from *doing/experience* to *reflection and analysis* of what was done to *planning* further interventions, which then results in future interventions/experience. Supervision is an important process that allows practitioners to stand back and *reflect on the intervention* that took place, the experience of the service user, and judgements that were made; to *evaluate* their own responses and the responses of the service user; to *reflect on alternative actions*; and to *make plans* for future interventions in line with the learning from this one.

Box 6.6 Reflecting on your practice in a particular intervention

It may be useful to draw on the following questions within supervision to help the process of reflection and analysis of a particular intervention/experience/event.

- What was your role?
- What were your aims for this piece of work/intervention?
- What expectations did you have?
- What concerns did you have?
- What happened, in your view?
- What happened, from a colleague's perspective?
- What observations did you make?
- What went well? What didn't?
- What do you think was the service user's view? Did you ask them for their thoughts/views?
- Describe the range of feelings you had?
- What feelings are you left with now?
- What aims or outcomes were not achieved?
- What theories/methods/approaches did you draw on?
- What legislation and/or policy is relevant to this situation?
- What alternative methods or approaches could have been tried?
- What are the possible risks and benefits in trying these alternatives?
- What needs to be done next?
- What would be your plan for future intervention?
- What are the goals of future intervention?
- What are the different ways you could approach the future intervention?
- What preparation could you do to support future intervention (e.g. increase knowledge of any legislation/policy/theory/methods)?
- What training or support needs has this raised for you?
- What steps can be taken to get any training/support identified?

Using these questions with your supervisor to explore a particular intervention or event may help you to focus on what happened and start the process of reflection and analysis that will support your learning and inform future interventions.

Source: adapted from Morrison 2005

Davys and Beddoe (2010) recognise the importance of 'strengths-based supervision' where supervision is future-focused and recognises supervisees as 'experts' about their own practice. They also consider that the driving force of supervision should be the 'experience of the learner (supervisee) and not the supervisor's knowledge' (Davys and Beddoe 2010, p.88).

The questions in Box 6.6 may help you to use supervision to reflect on your practice within a particular situation, and to reflect on alternative approaches to situations and future needs.

Banks (2009) stresses that one of the aims of supervision is to share mistakes and uncertainties about practice, and that if a practitioner is going to use supervision to reflect on and learn from mistakes, there needs to be a trusting relationship, and clear boundaries within that relationship. This leads us back to the importance of the supervision agreement and discussing expectations at the start of the supervisory relationship.

In the current climate of practice where risk assessment and quality assurance is of prime concern, there have been concerns expressed that supervision is now more underpinned by a performance management agenda and used for surveillance of practitioners (Gilbert 2001; Johns 2001; Peach and Horner 2007), which may threaten the idea of supervision as a learning-focused activity (Beddoe 2010). Therefore, creating an environment where you feel comfortable in reflecting on your practice and how things might have been done differently relies on the clear agreements and clarity around expectations that we have already discussed.

Managing tensions within supervision
There are many factors that may cause tension within the supervisory relationship, including:

- frustration at lack of resources
- unrealistic expectations
- heavy workload/stress at work
- personal difficulties impacting on work
- infrequent or cancelled supervision sessions

- conflict over agency or organisational changes and polices

- disagreement over the way forward for service users

- supervisee feeling criticised.

As stated throughout this chapter, supervision relies on an open, honest and trusting relationship between the supervisor and supervisee and therefore it is important to highlight any tensions as they arise, rather than dwell on them. It is important to recognise that receiving feedback on your practice is a useful part of your learning and development. However, this feedback needs to be clear, owned, regular, balanced and specific (Hawkins and Shohet 2006), and you need to be able to listen to the feedback without immediately becoming defensive, and to reflect on what you can learn from it.

Davys and Beddoe (2010) provide some useful guidelines to assist with receiving feedback:

- Ask for feedback directly.

- Discuss with your supervisor how you would like to receive feedback.

- First reflect on what you have done and evaluate your own performance.

- Ask for clarity/more information/more details if you feel the feedback is unclear.

- Make sure that you are receiving both positive and negative feedback, and separate the two.

It is important to have a process to evaluate the supervision you are receiving, and also for the supervisor to evaluate the supervision they are providing. You need to check out whether there is a formal process for evaluating and reviewing supervision arrangements, and whether there is a process for you to give feedback to your supervisor. There may be arrangements in place for occasional three-way meetings with another manager whose role is to join the supervision session and get feedback on the arrangements from both parties. In the early stages of a new supervisory relationship it maybe useful for you to review and evaluate supervision on a regular basis (i.e. at the end of each supervision session), and give feedback to each other and address any issues or changes for the next session.

It is important to remember that if you feel supervision is not working for you, then you have a responsibility to do something about it!

Supervision and working with ethical dilemmas

On a daily basis you meet questions about the best way to respond to situations, and you will also encounter competing views (your own and those of others). It is a really good use of supervision to talk through ethical dilemmas and weigh up competing views.

Golightley (2008) highlights 'culturally competent practice' within mental health practice, and the way our own stereotypical views, attitudes, values and beliefs can permeate professional practice. It is therefore important to recognise, question and reflect on our own attitudes, values and prejudices and how these may impact on our practice choices and decision making. Moving beyond our prejudices and stereotypes will help us develop practice responses that are 'culturally competent'.

Your values, knowledge base and previous experiences will also impact on the approaches and models that underpin your practice. It is also important to have a good understanding of a range of models and approaches that can inform the work with service users, and to reflect on your own practice and that of your team.

When working with adult client groups, especially within mental health, with older people, people with learning disabilities or physical disabilities, and within generic hospital settings, there are two main theoretical perspectives that will inform your work with service users: the *medical model* and the *social model*. It is important to reflect carefully on your own understanding of these two perspectives and how they can impact on service user assessment and decision making. As a social worker within adult services you can often find yourself within a medical setting, where the medical model predominates over your practice decisions. Whilst it is vital to have a clear understanding of medical approaches and treatments, reflecting on where you place the importance of social and environmental factors and causes, and recognising the impact of power and oppression, are essential in ensuring that you find the best possible way forward for the service user in question. Supervision can provide a useful opportunity to reflect on these issues, and also to discuss contexts where you may be working alongside colleagues who are approaching a situation from a different professional viewpoint.

Supervision can also be an important place to reflect upon the tensions that arise between 'care vs. control' and 'empowering vs. protective' practice. You will often be required to make decisions that challenge your social work values of empowerment, service user rights, and self-determination in order to ensure that a service user is protected (e.g. compulsory admission to hospital under the Mental Health Act; moving an older person with dementia into a nursing home; making decisions for a person with learning disabilities who cannot make the decision themselves). Supervision can support difficult decision making, allowing you space and time to reflect on the decisions you made and the feelings you have since experienced.

Box 6.7 Supervision activity

- Discuss in supervision the main theoretical approaches/perspectives/ models that are important in working with your client group.

- Identify how your own practice and value base fit into these approaches.

- Think of work with two service users where different approaches are drawn upon in the care plan – how does this work in practice, and what is your role?

Using supervision to support working across organisational and professional boundaries

Inquiries into high-profile child deaths (e.g. Victoria Climbié and Baby Peter Connelly), killings by mentally ill people (e.g. Christopher Clunis, John Barrett and Peter Bryan) and adult abuse cases (e.g. the Sutton and Merton inquiry into learning disability services, and the serious case review into the death of Steven Hoskin) all highlight failings in communication between professionals, agencies and organisations. They all raise issues about multi-agency working and collaboration and information-sharing.

While working in adult services, it is important to reflect on your role with other teams and/or organisations and on how you can use supervision to ensure clear communication and good working relationships with other professionals and professional groups. For example, your service user may be a parent, and although you focus on the parent's mental health or learning disability or health needs, you also have a key role in ensuring that the child's needs are met and that the child is appropriately protected from harm. This often raises conflict between, on the one hand, building a trusting relationship with your service user and supporting them in terms of their own needs, and on the other hand, needing to raise concerns about a child's welfare and their need for protection. Supervision can be a useful environment to reflect on the tensions in your own views and feelings, and also the tensions you may encounter when working alongside colleagues who are coming to the situation from a different perspective. Supervision can support you to balance these competing demands and deal appropriately with the dilemmas that arise in practice.

Becoming a supervisor

As you progress in your own career and develop your skills, knowledge and experience, you will start to move towards the role of supervising and teaching others and will need to be given opportunities to take on additional responsibility and contribute to the learning of colleagues. You will have moved through the stages of development (Hawkins and Shohet 2006) identified on page 110 and be at the 'process-in-context-centred (mature) stage' where you have reached professional maturity and can articulate professional knowledge and insight to others. Your own supervision will provide the forum to discuss your development into this new role and assist you to identify how it can be achieved (e.g. are there any training courses that would support you to take on the additional responsibility?). What support needs will you have in taking on additional responsibility? The interesting part of taking on this new role is the need to reflect on your own experiences of being supervised; your own expectations of supervision; your own learning styles and how these may impact on your style as a supervisor; and the methods and approaches you will draw on with a supervisee.

Key considerations

- It is widely recognised within the literature that supervision is central to social work and social care practice, regardless of the stage you are at in your career.

- As a starting point it is important to reflect on your own views and expectations around supervision, as these could impact on how you engage with the process and could prevent you from getting the most out of supervision.

- There is general agreement that a clear supervision contract or written agreement underpins good supervision. A contract identifies the structure, organisation and arrangements of supervision, identifies roles and responsibilities, considers the content of sessions and expectations, and provides a basis for reviewing the supervisory relationship.

- It is important to see supervision as much more than planned, formal, one-to-one sessions, recognising that unplanned and *ad hoc* supervision with your supervisor should be a normal part of the supervisory relationship.

- It is important to have a process to evaluate the supervision you are receiving, and also for the supervisor to evaluate the supervision they are providing.

Chapter 7

Managing Stress

- What is work-related stress?
- Identifying stressors
- Signs and symptoms
- Managing stress: coping mechanisms
- Developing stress resilience

The Health and Safety Executive (HSE) defines work-related stress as:

> The adverse reaction people have to excessive pressures or other types of demand placed on them at work... Stress is not an illness – it is a state. However, if stress becomes too excessive or too prolonged, mental and physical illness may develop. (HSE 2011)

The HSE acknowledges that generally work is good for us and that a certain amount of pressure at work can be a 'positive and motivating' factor. However, it is when the pressure becomes overwhelming that stress occurs. 'Stress is a natural reaction to too much pressure' (HSE 2011).

There has been public acknowledgement of the stressful and complex nature of social work and the demands and pressures facing the profession, and this is reinforced in the final report of the Social Work Task Force (2009), which recommends a comprehensive reform of the profession.

Why is it important to be aware of work-related stress and how to manage it?

You will already be very familiar with stress, having just completed your three-year degree, and it is likely that you will have developed your own coping strategies, some healthy and some unhealthy, to deal with it! A never-ending barrage of assignment deadlines, placement pressures and the everyday challenges that life throws at you will be all too familiar. However, it is likely that you will have coped with this to some extent by knowing that it would be time-limited. However, as you start the next stage of your professional life, it is important to develop good, healthy coping strategies which will help to sustain you through the inevitable demands, pressures and stressors that you will experience at different stages in your career. These strategies will take a number of forms: some will be formal and structured (such as regular and effective supervision), and others more informal (such as finding time to relax and reflect). You will draw on a range of resources, including your personal qualities, as well as developing good skills such as effective time management and organisational skills.

There has been a recruitment and retention problem for a significant period of time in social work and this has been attributed in part to high levels of stress and burnout amongst workers. Assisting social workers at all levels of their career in managing stress is very much on the social work agenda, in terms both of supporting NQSWs and of addressing some key factors which have been identified by the Social Work Task Force, such as too much form filling and bureaucracy, high caseloads and organisational change.

Identifying stressors

Take a moment to write down some of the things which have made you feel anxious and unable to cope.

Box 7.1 Identifying stressors: Activity 1

- What happened?
- How did it make you feel?
- What did you do about it?
- How do you feel about it now?

As an NQSW you have to cope with the transition from student to qualified professional, and this is sometimes a scary prospect. You may experience very different expectations of you now that you are qualified, and this can be daunting. 'Role ambiguity' can be defined as 'a lack of clarity about what is expected of you' and is a recognised stress factor, particularly when you are newly qualified (Chang and Hancock 2003). It is possible, although not inevitable, that in the early days of your first qualified post, you may feel that you lack adequate knowledge and skills to perform the tasks required of you, and it is important at this stage to be realistic in your expectations of yourself, as well as realistic in your expectations of others. It is also possible that the reality of the job does not match your preconceptions about the role and that you may, as a result, be feeling anxious about whether or not you have made the right career decision. Public perceptions of the social work profession, fuelled by often hostile media, can also contribute to negative feelings about your role. However, Huxley *et al.* (2005) concluded from a study into stress and pressure in mental health social workers that 'there is enjoyment in relationships and working with people and there is high intrinsic job satisfaction' (Collins 2008, p.1176). There may be constraints which work against this, as reflected in the Social Work Reform Board's finding that high levels of paperwork and data input means that time spent in direct contact with service users has been significantly eroded. It is positive that this has been acknowledged and it is to be hoped that it will improve in the future.

Although your team will be aware of your newly qualified status and structures will have been (should have been) put in place to support you, it is important to understand that in the hurly-burly of everyday practice, you need to be proactive in seeking support. Your colleagues are not mindreaders and cannot guess how you are feeling. Don't be afraid to ask questions, even if it is the hundredth you have asked that day! Everyone was in your position at some point.

Stress can also occur when you have too little to do, which can lead to an individual feeling deskilled and devalued. You may experience this for a short time before you get into the swing of things within your new team. Make the most of it to familiarise yourself with policy and procedure, and perhaps in getting to know the geographical area. It is unlikely to last long!

Social work by its very nature can be stressful because you will be dealing with other people's stress when they are particularly vulnerable, and you may be in a position of gatekeeping very scarce resources, which can lead to frustration and anger. The responsibilities and powers which are part of your professional role can weigh heavily on you as an individual because you will be part of making life-changing decisions for vulnerable people, albeit decisions that will be made in partnership with individual service users, their families and carers, as well as other professionals.

An identified stress factor in social work is the ongoing context of uncertainty and change, driven by external factors such as social, political and cultural shifts, leading to changing policy and legislation. The change process can sometimes appear to be continuous with no time for policy and procedure to be embedded before the next change occurs. A seemingly constant process of restructuring and reorganisation coupled with increasing budgetary constraints can be destabilising and demoralizing and can leave individuals, teams and services generally in a state of anxiety and distress. Understanding the context of your work and what is driving the changes can be helpful in managing the uncertainty and approaching change in a positive and constructive way (Johnson and Williams 2007).

Stress inevitably affects people in different ways, and as your career progresses you are likely to experience periods when you are more sensitive to some stressful situations than others. This is often dependent on where you are in your personal life at any one time. Being self-aware is very important because this can help you plan for how to manage potential stress factors in your professional life. What people perceive to be stressful will also vary from person to person and can depend on many factors, including:

- your background and culture
- skills and experience
- personality
- personal circumstances
- individual characteristics
- health status

- ethnicity, gender, age or disability
- other demands both inside and outside work.

(HSE 2011)

Box 7.2 Identifying stressors: Activity 2

Think about how any of the factors listed above might impact on the way that you perceive and manage stressful situations.

" When my mum was terminally ill, I found it difficult to deal with other people's distress when I was feeling so bad myself. (NQSW) "

Remember, everyone is different, and experiencing stress is not a sign of weakness.

How do I know I am suffering from stress? What are the signs and symptoms?

Donnellan and Jack (2010) highlight that stress does not necessarily lead to ill health but can have a number of negative consequences, including poor decision making, 'presenteeism' or absenteeism, and burnout.

Early negative signs of stress which will impact on decision making might include:

- loss of concentration
- an inability to handle new information
- an increased tendency to procrastinate or postpone activities
- hasty decision making or 'panicked' choices
- oversimplification of alternatives
- a reduction in creative thinking
- more defensiveness about your decisions
- more irrational or hostile feelings
- increasing withdrawal and social isolation.

(Donnellan and Jack 2010, p.113)

131

Clearly the consequences of any of the above will increase risk to service users, as well as to the social worker.

The Health and Safety Executive gives guidance on other symptoms to be aware of.

Box 7.3 Symptoms of stress

Emotional symptoms

- negative or depressive feeling
- disappointment with yourself
- increased emotional reactions – more tearful or sensitive or aggressive
- loneliness, withdrawn
- loss of motivation, commitment and confidence
- mood swings (not behavioural)

Mental symptoms

- confusion, indecision
- can't concentrate
- poor memory

Changes from your normal behaviour

- changes in eating habits
- increased smoking, drinking or drug taking 'to cope'
- mood swings affecting your behaviour
- changes in sleep patterns
- twitchy, nervous behaviour
- changes in attendance such as arriving later or taking more time off

Please note these are indicators of behaviour of those experiencing stress. They may also be indicative of other conditions. If you are concerned about yourself please seek advice from your GP. If you are concerned about a colleague try to convince them to see their GP.

Source: HSE 2011

These symptoms are clues and can creep up on you; you may be unaware of them in yourself but may in fact notice them in others. If you are experiencing any of the symptoms above over a prolonged period of time, it is important to seek help and advice.

Donnellan and Jack (2010) draw on the work of Cooper and Rousseau (2001) and the concept of 'presenteeism' to highlight the consequences of the 'inappropriate non-use of sick leave' or, in other words, coming to work when you are unwell. This may occur in organisations where there is a culture in which acknowledging that you are suffering from stress will be viewed negatively and as a sign of weakness, and may have long-term implications for future promotion. Donnellan and Jack highlight the irony of this for organisations, in that the consequences are likely to be a longer term of absence as a result of 'burnout', which will have a knock-on impact on remaining staff and on morale and staff retention generally.

Freudenberger and Richelson (1980) define burnout as a psychological response to 'long-term exhaustion and diminished interest' and highlight that it is not a condition that gets better by being ignored. Even if you hold fears that taking time off work because of stress will be viewed negatively by your organisation, it is important that you ultimately take responsibility for your own health and well-being.

How to manage stress in the workplace

Coping mechanisms

We all develop our own coping mechanisms, some helpful and some less helpful and even destructive. From the personal experience of one of the authors as a social worker, a well-known coping strategy is the consumption of copious amounts of cake, and the sight of a colleague returning from a visit clutching a bag of doughnuts from the local one-stop shop was a signal to put the kettle on!

Lazarus (1998) defines coping as:

> The person's constantly changing cognitive and behavioural efforts to meet specific external and/or internal demands that are appraised as taxing or exceeding the resources of the person. (p.202)

Collins (2008) identifies two different ways of coping:

- *Vigilant coping*: this demands a degree of problem solving or active coping, looking at ways to prevent, reduce or control the source of stress.

- *Emotion focused coping*: which is a way of reducing or managing stress, usually in the type of situation where the cause of stress cannot be prevented and must be endured.

(Collins 2008, p.1177)

Box 7.4 Two different ways of coping with stress

- Think about occasions or situations you have experienced which required either of the two different ways of coping defined above.
- Think about the processes involved in the two different ways of coping and the types of support that you drew on.
- Were these internal or external supports?

“ I often feel overwhelmed and that I don't know if I am doing or saying the right thing. My manager is very supportive. (NQSW) **”**

Poor coping strategies

Collins (2008) identifies two potentially dysfunctional strategies as behavioural and mental disengagement.

- *Behavioural disengagement* involves withdrawing from the potentially stressful situation, which might mean 'adopting a position of helplessness', such as putting the responsibility onto someone else. An example might be making appointments at times when you know the service user is unlikely to be at home, or simply putting things off and avoiding the situation. Most experienced social workers will own up to having felt huge relief when they turn up for a potentially difficult visit to find no one at home! If this is how you are feeling, it is important not to bury your head in the sand but to acknowledge those feelings and seek support.

- *Mental disengagement* involves avoidance activities which enable you to distance yourself from the situation you are finding stressful. Carver, Scheier and Weintraub (1989) include activities like 'excessive drinking, drug use, wishful thinking, day dreaming and inappropriate sleeping' (quoted in Collins 2008, p.1178). These are all symptoms of stress identified by the Health and Safety Executive (2011).

Denial is another potentially dysfunctional or negative coping strategy. Most of us can think of occasions when someone may have asked us if we are coping and we have said 'Yes' but really meant 'No, I need help.' As mentioned already, your colleagues and line managers or friends and family members cannot read your mind, although they may have picked up on clues that you are not managing and may be feeling out of your depth. However, it is your responsibility to ask for help and to understand that experiencing stress is not a weakness. Denying or internalising a problem is not helpful for your own well-being, is potentially risky for colleagues and service users, and will only displace the problem until a later date (Collins 2008).

Support

Why is support so important in managing stress? We have already identified unhelpful coping strategies, which tend to involve internalising the distress in different ways. Using support networks serves two valuable purposes (Carver *et al.* 1989).

The first is that it offers the opportunity to take advice to assist planning and problem solving and is likely to involve formal support. This correlates with the 'vigilant coping' model (Collins 2008). Kinman and Grant (2010) highlight the importance of the provision of effective reflective supervision, which offers the opportunity for trainees or NQSWs to manage complex social work cases and learn from practice experience. Reflective supervision should be an opportunity to learn more about yourself, your skills, competences and developmental needs, and how to manage your emotional responses to your work. It is important for you as an NQSW to understand the importance of this type of supervision and to take some responsibility for ensuring that supervision is not purely about case management. Kinman and Grant (2010) see this type of supervision as 'key to building resilience and managing stressful work' (Community Care 2010b). (For a more detailed look at the importance of good supervision, refer to Chapter 6.)

The second valuable purpose of support is that it addresses an emotional need for reassurance and 'moral support', and is likely to be an immediate opportunity to debrief after a stressful experience. This correlates with Collins' (2008) emotion-focused model. This opportunity would normally be provided informally by colleagues who are around at the time and provides a way of letting go of some of the stress and anxiety you are feeling, which can prevent it being internalised and, which is even more important, will stop you taking it all home with you. This type of support should be a two-way or reciprocal process and is invaluable in that it provides an opportunity to talk to someone who is not a manager but is nevertheless someone who understands the pressures of the job and the types of situation you have experienced. Using support in this way helps you to leave those feelings at work and not let them spill over into your family or social life.

It is important to remember that the types of issues that you have become accustomed to dealing with professionally are not part of everyone's experience, and sometimes well-meaning attempts by family or friends to reassure you might exacerbate the stress you are experiencing. Feeling misunderstood is not helpful and can lead to conflict in your personal relationships. If this opportunity to talk or debrief is not available to you because there is no one around to talk to, it is sometimes useful to write a few things down and use this as a way of detaching, before going home. In good supportive teams, colleagues make it their business to be aware if someone has a potentially difficult visit at the end of the day and will be happy to talk to you if necessary. (You should also make yourself aware of the lone working policy and make sure that you use it appropriately.) You may have been provided with a mentor or have set up a 'buddy' system which provides you with support at work. You cannot always assume that there is a culture of informal support within a team, but there is nothing to stop you being proactive in encouraging this.

It is important to be mindful that there have to be boundaries. Constantly seeking reassurance and wanting to talk about things can make it hard to work through the distress towards a more problem-solving approach, so a balance must be sought.

The support of family and friends can come in the form of emotional or practical help and can be important in getting things into perspective and achieving a healthy work–life balance. Having interests and hobbies is a healthy way of balancing the pressures of work and gives you the opportunity to detach from the stresses of your working life.

> Ensuring that you take time out to relax and be mindful of the world around you is essential. Learning to be fully present in the moment rather than rushing from one crisis to the next can really help to enhance the way you manage stress. (Community Care 2010b)

Developing stress resilience

Recent research undertaken by the University of Bedford has looked specifically at 'the development of structures to support the work-related well-being of trainee social workers' and to encourage and promote 'stress resilience' (Kinman and Grant 2010, p.2).

Much of the discourse around resilience relates to how children cope with adversity. Gilligan (1997) offers a definition as:

> qualities which cushion a vulnerable child from the worst effects of adversity in whatever form it takes and which may help a child or young person to cope, survive, and even thrive in the face of great hurt and disadvantage. (Gilligan 1997, p.12)

Theories of resilience have been developed and applied to other situations, including work-related stress (Howard in Kinman and Grant 2008).

Factors associated with resilience in children come under three categories:

- psychological/dispositional attributes
- family support and cohesion
- external support systems.
>   (Friborg et al. 2003)

We have already looked at the second and third of these factors in relation to coping with work-related stress, and we will now consider the importance of psychological and dispositional attributes.

Kinman and Grant (2010) propose that 'emotional intelligence, reflective ability, aspects of empathy and social competence may be the key protective qualities in the social care context' (p.10). Morrison

(2006) discusses the relevance of emotional intelligence (EI) in social work practice, including in the management of stress. So what is EI? Goleman (1996) defines it as:

> Being able to motivate oneself and persist in the face of frustrations: to control impulse and delay gratification; to regulate one's moods and keep distress from swamping the ability to think; to empathize and to hope. (Goleman 1996, cited in Morrison 2007, p.2)

Morrison (2007) reflects on his own observations of the growing importance of EI in social work over recent years and notes that it distinguishes those practitioners who 'display a congruence of professional, academic and personal mindfulness that sets them apart from their competent colleagues' (p.3). He notes that some of the characteristics of EI or emotional competence as having the ability to engage in individual reflection and demonstrate 'accurate empathy, self awareness and self management skills'. Much of the discourse around EI focuses on the importance of relationship-based social work practice and the role of EI in developing human relationships between the social worker and service user to promote change and enhanced well-being (Platt 2003; Trevithick 2003).

Theories around EI grew out of the notion that there are different forms of intelligence and that an emphasis on cognitive intelligence is a poor predictor of how individuals will perform in both their personal and professional lives. Academic success does not give any guarantee that an individual will be fully equipped for their chosen career, particularly if the role involves communication and engagement with others. Most theories of EI are based on a four-domain, interconnected model, as represented in Figure 7.1.

You will note that in Figure 7.1 there are two intrapersonal domains: self-awareness and self-management, and two interpersonal domains: awareness of others/empathy and relationship skills (Morrison 2006). This could be summarised as a strong indicator that in order to be in touch with a service user's feelings, a practitioner also has to be self-aware (Shulman 1999).

Research has demonstrated that professionals with low EI and poor social skills are more likely to experience high levels of stress and 'burnout' than those with higher levels. However, high levels of EI do not necessarily protect individuals from burnout.

Intrapersonal intelligence   Interpersonal intelligence

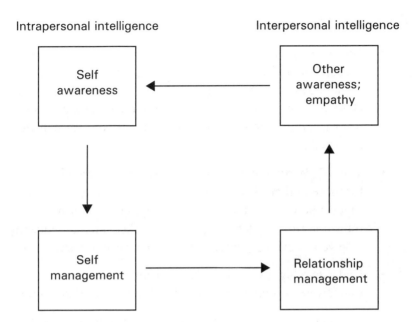

Figure 7.1 The four-domain model of emotional intelligence
Source: adapted from Morrison 2007

Empathy or empathetic concern is generally seen as an ability to share and understand another person's feelings, and as vital for social workers to possess in order to be able to acknowledge and accept what their service users are thinking and feeling. However, it is extremely important to ensure that there are clear boundaries around this, and that empathetic concern does not spill over into empathetic distress when witnessing the distress of others becomes painful and distressing for the worker (see Davis 1983, cited in Kinman and Grant 2010). Demonstrating an over-identification with the service user's distress is likely to exacerbate their feelings of helplessness and will undermine your professional role. Research has shown that being able to feel appropriate empathy enhances stress resilience, whereas empathetic distress can reduce it significantly.

It is important to point out here that social workers are human and there will be certain situations to which you are more sensitive than others because they perhaps resonate with something in your personal or professional life. This is where EI and reflective ability are vital to enable you to seek appropriate support.

Key considerations

- Social work has been acknowledged to be a stressful occupation, and therefore experiencing stress is not a sign of weakness but a natural response to the demands of your role. However, not everyone will respond in the same way to stress factors, and it is not inevitable that you will experience distress as a result.

- The NQSW programme has been developed to provide support for those in their first year of practice. It should put in place a support network to assist you in managing the demands of the transition from student to qualified worker, and consequently help you to manage stress in a constructive and positive way.

- Understanding and being able to identify stressors is the first step towards managing stress and seeking appropriate support.

- It is important to acknowledge and express how you are feeling, in both formal and informal settings. Other people cannot read your mind and you must take personal responsibility for seeking support.

- The negative consequences of stress can creep up on you slowly. It is important to understand the signs and address them at the earliest opportunity in order to avoid burnout.

- Ensure that you understand the difference between helpful and unhelpful coping strategies and are confident in using those that are helpful.

- Identify and use support networks appropriately.

- It is possible to develop stress resilience. Key factors in this are reflective ability and emotional intelligence. These are skills which can be developed.

- A manageable amount of stress can be good for you because it keeps you focused and interested in what you are doing.

Chapter 8

Continuing Professional Development, Critical Reflection and Building for the Future

∴ Continuing professional development (CPD) in context

∴ Lifelong learning and education

∴ Using experience in critical reflection

∴ CPD pathways for me

Learning throughout life

> **"** My advice would be to keep knowledge up to date and don't be afraid of learning! (NQSW) **"**

Learning is an activity we all engage in throughout our lives and is part of everyday living. We develop the necessary skills required to live our lives by combining our life knowledge with life experience. As adults we learn to manage situations, at work and in our domestic settings, that as children or young adults we could never have conceived of. The motivation to engage in further learning frequently occurs as we enter new social roles – for example, as a wage earner, homeowner, partner or parent. Such continued learning is often informal in nature and will appear as a natural process as we mature. However, skills to cope with everyday life will have evolved from a continued process of knowledge and experience interacting with one another.

Just as this process has enabled you to develop new skills and knowledge in your social and personal life, the same will be expected to do this in your professional life. There is an expectation that as a professional social worker you will continue to engage in learning to further the development of your professional skills, and to achieve this you will need to blend both learned and experiential theory and knowledge with practice.

Rolfe, Freshwater and Jasper (2001) provide a useful framework which conceptualises the interrelationship between theory, knowledge, experience, practice and learning.

A model of learning, knowledge and practice

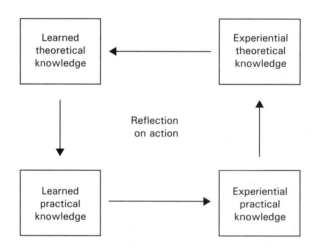

Figure 8.1 The relationship between theory, knowledge, experience, practice and learning
Source: adapted from Rolfe, Freshwater and Jasper 2001

- *Learned theoretical knowledge*: as a practitioner you acquire a body of knowledge through academic studies, attending training sessions, books, assignment writing, exams and presentations. Through supervised practice you learn to transfer theory into practice.

- *Learned practical knowledge*: the practitioner develops a body of practical knowledge in the form of policy, legislation, research and procedures. This knowledge is stored in the brain and is easily accessed to support practice, and easily articulated in words. At the same time as internalising some of this practical knowledge, you begin to act without consciously thinking about what you are doing. You also begin to modify some of this practical knowledge to meet the requirements of real life situations.

- *Experiential practical knowledge*: eventually, after much experience, you almost reject the learned practical knowledge in favour of experiential practical knowledge. This body of knowledge is largely organismic, stored in the muscles and reflexes (i.e. gut feeling) and is very difficult to articulate. You do the right thing but are sometimes unable to readily say how and why it is the right thing to do. Although you are no longer drawing explicitly on theoretical and practical learning, it is not lost, but available when faced with a novel situation.

- *Experiential theoretical knowledge*: through reflection, the practitioner begins to recognise, understand and articulate the processes underpinning his or her expertise. You begin to understand the rational process that underpins intuition. You begin to build a body of experiential practical knowledge. This is not the content-based knowledge of a beginner, but rather a process-based knowledge, which is concerned with how and why you practice, rather than what you practice. Furthermore, it can be shared between practitioners, transcends professional boundaries and is common to all practice-based disciplines.

This model provides some clarity on the process of learning. Learning should be viewed not as a one-off event but as something you do throughout your career; indeed the cycle should continue for as long as you are in practice.

It will have already become apparent to you since qualification that social work is a profession that calls for continuing and consistent learning, and that this requires commitment and motivation on your part. Social work is a valuable and demanding occupation, and engaging in learning to improve your professional competence can be a challenge in terms of time and energy; therefore it is advisable to think clearly about why you need to engage in CPD, what CPD is, and what 'learning' you need to engage in to maximise your professional development.

Why CPD?

Engaging in CPD provides a framework and process to facilitate the combining of theory, experience and practice to achieve continued learning. This continuity of learning is important because, whilst you will already have begun to develop your competence and confidence as a practitioner, the nature of social work practice is such that you will frequently be faced with higher levels of complexity and increased levels of professional responsibility, which will call for higher levels of capability. Social work is not a profession that stands still, not least because of the evolutionary nature of social work roles and tasks that are subject to wider factors, such as the influence of government and society, which redefine the parameters of the relationship between the state, families and individuals, leading to new modes of service development and delivery. (See Chapter 5 for discussion of the professional role and task.)

Change can occur at such a pace in practice that you might sometimes feel overwhelmed and begin to question your role or purpose, leading you to respond to, rather than understand, the purpose of change. New directions in practice can also call for new ways of working or for old ways to be readjusted. Research that supported initial practice can become distant or outdated and practice can begin to take on a 'routine' feel. Working in such an environment can lead individuals to experience loss of confidence or lowering of self-esteem and feelings of frustration at the changing direction of professional practice. Sustained periods like this can lead to stress and burnout, and practice can become process-driven, with professionals beginning to forget why they came into the profession in the first place, thus losing those intrinsic motivational factors that are able to sustain you in the long term.

CPD provides a route you can use to mitigate such difficulties. Ironically, the emphasis on practitioners completing their CPD for the purpose of registration can be yet another of those changes that begin to feel like a pressure, and engagement in CPD could become tokenistic, when in reality most would agree that it is vitally important both for you and for those you work with. This is why it is important to understand the purpose of CPD and learn how to use it positively, right from the start of your career.

Recognition of the need for practitioners to participate in learning activities throughout their careers has increased since the early 1990s, as government, employers and employees have identified the value of CPD for social workers in the UK (Pietroni 1991). CPD activity is linked to issues of recruitment, retention and regulation within the social work profession. As discussed in Chapter 5, evidence from a range of industries shows that accessible career pathways and continuing professional development opportunities are critical in retaining staff and creating a motivated and stable workforce. Alongside this, the importance of CPD in supporting and regulating the social work profession has become more apparent following high-profile cases, such as the murder of Steven Hoskin, a man with a learning disability who lived in Cornwall. A variety of professionals, and the organisations they work for, were found to lack the necessary skills and knowledge to safeguard Steven from harm.

CPD provides one of the pathways used by successive governments to quality-assure professional practice, by making it a requirement for practitioners to take some responsibility in developing the skills and knowledge necessary to deliver effective and efficient services. The Social Work Reform Board has placed a clear emphasis on CPD in the context of the Professional Capabilities Framework (PCF), which provides an overarching structure covering key areas of practice (SWRB 2011). This provides you with a rationale and map from which you can navigate your engagement with CPD.

It is important to emphasise that, whilst such frameworks and expectations on the part of government and employer are central, of equal, if not more, importance is your personal and professional commitment to achieve the highest level of competence you can – not only for your own personal satisfaction or professional advancement, but also to provide the highest level of service possible for those individuals with whom you work, both now and in the future.

What is CPD?

CPD is simply a process that contributes to professional and personal development, and should be viewed as part of a framework that draws on knowledge and experience to develop lifelong learning. CPD is about identifying gaps in our knowledge and skills and seeking opportunities to develop new learning to fill those spaces (although learning may also sometimes require us to 'unlearn' first). What do we mean by this? Just think about driving a vehicle – who, as an experienced driver, could pass a driving test if asked to resit it right now? The chances are, many would consider they would not pass if put in such a position because they acknowledge that they have learnt a lot of bad habits that would contribute to failing a driving test; yet that will not stop that individual driving today and getting from A to B without incident. To pass another driving test we would probably have to unlearn some of those bad habits, and the way in which we would do this is to stop and think about what we are doing and revisit the right way of doing things, with some guidance from an instructor. Practice can be a bit like this; we can pick up bad habits when we continue to work in the same environment in the same way, day in and day out. Working for long periods of time without CPD can lead to the development of 'bad' habits in our practice, which in the short term may do no harm, but in the longer term create a foundation for day-to-day practice that could eventually lead to mechanistic and poor practice becoming the 'norm'.

Therefore engagement in CPD should be viewed as an activity that continues throughout your professional life. Attaining your professional qualification was the starting point, not an end.

What is lifelong learning?

'Lifelong learning' relates to the enabling process that develops individuals' abilities 'to do' tasks (Delors *et al.* 1996). Some differentiate between lifelong learning and lifelong education, suggesting that the former is focused on developing vocational skills and knowledge via attendance at non-accredited training events, whereas the latter is understood as engaging in learning that is accredited and designed to enable the individual to be more critical, analytical and socio-political in nature (Grace 2004). Both are of equal value and will be required at different times throughout your career.

In terms of planning for the future you will probably need to access a variety of learning opportunities that meet both your educational and vocational needs, so it is useful to consider the purpose of any CPD activity before participating, to ensure that you engage in the form most appropriate to meet your professional needs' (see Table 8.1).

Table 8.1 CPD for specific vocational requirements

CPD activity	CPD purpose
Post Qualifying (PQ) Higher Specialist Award in Mental Health Practice (provided by university programme).	Enables practitioner to meet statutory requirements to act as Advanced Mental Health Practitioner (AMHP).
Safeguarding Adults Investigator training (provided by in-house or commissioned trainer).	Enables practitioner to meet requirements of local authority employer to act a Safeguarding Adults investigator.
Mental Capacity Act 2005 training (provided by in-house or commissioned trainer).	Enables practitioner to develop skills and knowledge in applying legislation to practice.
Best Interest Assessor for the Deprivation of Liberty Safeguards (DoLS) (provided by university programme).	Enables practitioner to meet the Department of Health regulatory requirements for statutory role of Best Interest Assessor under the Deprivation of Liberty Safeguards (DoLS).
Application of eligibility criteria (in-house training).	Enables practitioner to understand and apply local and national policy to practice.

CPD Pathways

CPD should be a continuous process that contributes to your current and future professional and personal developmental needs; therefore you need to think about, and plan ahead to decide, what type of CPD is most appropriate to help you achieve your goals.

There is no one way to engage in CPD, as demonstrated in Table 8.1. However, it is generally acknowledged that CPD has three main routes:

- *Formal learning*: leading to recognised awards and post-qualifying qualifications.

- *Informal learning*: in-house workshops, induction, self-directed learning (online, for example).

- *Experiential learning*: job swaps, mentoring, shadowing.

These can be provided by a variety of organisations and individuals, such as universities, training companies, training departments, service users and carers, peers, social work students, and other professionals. There is no hierarchy in these; each has an important role and they can be mixed-and-matched. For example, formal learning may be assessed or unassessed (e.g. AMHP training or Safeguarding Investigator training – both equip the practitioner to undertake a particular role in their organisation; however, the first is formally assessed by a university, the other is not). Experiential learning might be formally organised by your employer but informal in its application – for example, shadowing a senior team member, presenting research at a team meeting, or running a journal club.

The thing to remember is, where possible try and be creative in engaging in CPD. A variety of approaches is more likely to stimulate you than taking the same approach all of the time.

Partnership working in CPD

To participate on any of these routes requires some degree of partnership involving three main groups:

1. practitioners

2. employer

3. providers of CPD activity.

It will also probably involve many others frequently not identified within literature around CPD, such as friends, family and peers. All may somehow be affected by your pursuit of CPD, and all may have a key role in supporting you. These are often the 'hidden' partnerships that, whilst not acknowledged in professional literature, often provide the foundation that enables you to pursue CPD. Whilst the focus of this chapter is on the three main groups, some of the general principles of good partnership working are equally applicable to these less obvious partnerships. For a partnership approach in CPD to work, there needs to be trust between partners, and each needs to have realistic expectations of the other. The activity you are going to engage in as CPD also needs to be relevant, and there should be equality in ability to access CPD opportunities within your organisation. Without these CPD could become exhausting rather than enhancing.

Practitioners, employers and providers of CPD each have a distinctive role to play in the CPD process. It is useful to keep in mind these roles and responsibilities as you seek to engage with CPD activity.

CPD: roles and responsibilities

Practitioner

In effect, *you!* It is your responsibility to take a proactive approach to engaging in and formulating learning activities. This is a shift from viewing skills and knowledge development as something done to the practitioner. Some CPD will be dependent on the support and requirements of the employer and/or the provider of CPD activity – for example, in terms of entry requirements for a formal academic course, or designated period of practice experience before being allowed to undertake particular training or role within your employing organisation. However, learning activities also need to be driven by you to ensure that you meet any registration requirements, as well as your professional and personal CPD needs, to facilitate your development.

CPD is also linked to your professional registration. A condition of registration renewal is that social workers maintain their competence to practise, and this is evidenced through PRTL. It is the registrant's (your) responsibility to demonstrate, and record, any CPD activity that may contribute to PRTL.

Employer

At a regulatory level there is an expectation that CPD activities will be consistent with the aims and objectives of the employer and their organisation; therefore employers should provide CPD opportunities that enable practitioners to meet those requirements. It is a requirement in the profession's regulatory body's code of practice for social work employers to ensure that training and development opportunities are provided, so that social workers are equipped and prepared to meet their roles and responsibilities in practice. Employers should provide CPD opportunities to meet both personal and professional needs jointly identified under job appraisal systems, supervision, NQSW frameworks or induction programmes. Your line manager/supervisor has a critical role in actively contributing to identifying and supporting you in meeting your CPD needs.

Employers should also provide support to practitioners in their pursuit of CPD; this might include study leave, mentoring or financial support.

Providers

Providers of CPD activity have a responsibility to develop learning opportunities that meet practitioners' professional needs and employers' organisational needs in an effective and empowering manner. Therefore, you should expect the delivery of CPD activity (i.e. training/education) to be structured, clear, concise, of good quality and contemporary.

The partnerships discussed above exist at an organisational and personal level – for example, between your employer and your local university or independent training provider. However, more often than not, what really makes a difference in developing good partnerships is the effectiveness of those one-to-one or individual relationships.

Forming partnerships therefore requires seeking out relevant individuals and establishing an appropriate working relationship with them. It also makes a difference if you have confidence in those who provide CPD. This might mean meeting with your training department, or asking that your local provider of formal or informal training/ education be invited to provide information sessions to practitioners on the nature and quality of their provision, before committing to a course of study. It is useful, before enrolling on programmes that require an assessment of your work (for example, to attain an award or qualification of some sort), to meet those who will be delivering the training/education and those who will be assessing you.

The quality of relationship between you and each partner can help to ensure the quality of the support you will receive and the quality of CPD delivered. This might be a new approach for some you work with; however, it is important that you take a lead and actively engage in this process to maximise the potential outcomes of any CPD activity.

How do I identify my CPD needs?

Clearly, identifying the gaps in your skills and knowledge is central to deciding what your CPD needs are, for carrying out the roles and tasks expected of you by your employer currently, as well as for planning for your future. The first task is to review your personal and professional developmental needs in the context of your organisation's operational needs.

Using the NQSW framework

The NQSW framework provides a guide for your first year in practice to support the transition from student to professional social worker. A focus on your professional development will have played a central role, and can be used to plan and facilitate your CPD activity after your first year in practice. For an NQSW, induction, supervision and any appraisal system put in place by your employer should have included discussions about your ongoing learning and developmental needs. These will also have been recorded by you and your employer. Use them to provide a foundation from which to identify your CPD needs.

Using post-registration training and learning

You will also have engaged in training and learning in your first year of practice, which will have been recorded for the purpose of evidencing PRTL. This can provide vital information for identifying gaps in skills and knowledge, as well as tracking your developmental journey so far, and is therefore very useful in identifying the skills and knowledge you might need to develop in the future.

PRTL is a central requirement of registration as a social worker. The requirements of PRTL vary, depending on which country in the UK you are registered in. Therefore you need to check the requirements with your regulatory body (see Appendix I). Whilst it is primarily your responsibility to ensure that you meet any requirements and record your activity, your employer also has a role in providing CPD opportunities and recording your engagement in those activities. Your employer will have policy and procedures in place regarding PRTL, which you need to be familiar with. The recording of your PRTL activity is a key document that you can use to identify your CPD needs.

The key points to remember about PRTL are:

- Participating in, and recording of PRTL is the registrant's responsibility.

- PRTL can be made up of a range of CPD activities, i.e. formal/informal learning; experiential learning.

- PRTL should be the outcome of learning and developmental activities recognised in collaboration between employer and employee as relevant and appropriate.

- PRTL provides evidence of continued professional development of your professional capabilities and competence, to your regulatory body, employer, the individuals you work with, peers, government and wider society.

Box 8.1 The journey so far...

Use the following questions to begin to map your CPD journey so far:

- What types of CPD activities have I engaged in?
- What difference did these make to my professional development?
- What types of activities do I need to engage in in the future?
- How do I think these will facilitate my professional development?
- How and where can I access these?

There is a lot of flexibility in PRTL with which you can work. For example, time spent on PRTL activities can range from extended formal modules of study to whole or half-day training sessions or shadowing and mentoring experiences. The central tenet of any activity you participate in to demonstrate PRTL is that it must be meaningful and of benefit to your employer, yourself and the development and delivery of efficient and effective service provision to those you work with. Keep these aspects in mind and ensure that attendance at training and learning events are for these purposes, or engagement might become tokenistic, just to meet regulatory requirements rather than to seek true professional development.

Next steps

CPD is clearly not just about your future career development, although that is important; it has a much wider function in terms of meeting the needs of those individuals you work with and the organisations you work in, and as such is an important area to think about and engage in. CPD involves more than updating oneself on the latest policy and guidance from your employer or government on 'how' to do something, which (although also important) is not the only function of CPD. CPD also needs to enable you to develop a broader knowledge and deeper understanding of the 'why's' of doing. Simply just 'doing' the job and responding to change will only demotivate and deskill practitioners in the longer term, if they are unable to locate practice in some form of context.

Training events and vocational learning designed to meet the operational needs of the organisation you work in probably formed the core of your CPD activity in the first year of practice. This will have proved extremely useful as you got to grips with the technicalities of day-to-day practice, and will also have contributed to enabling you to meet any NQSW requirements. However, once through the initial year of practice you might begin to consider what forms of CPD you need to engage in as part of a career development strategy for the next two to five years.

Whilst the wider context clearly has some influence over the content, structure and purpose of CPD, it is useful to remember that CPD is not just about training and educating you to meet targets, competencies and capabilities, but also has a personal and socially transformative purpose.

- *Personal function*: increases individuals' confidence and self-esteem.

- *Socially transformative*: challenges the status quo.

It is important to have a balanced view of the purpose of CPD if you are going to engage in it meaningfully and get maximum impact from it. Continually engaging in learning that is unfulfilling and meaningless will ultimately demotivate you. Think back to Chapter 5, where we identified 'extrinsic' factors as important in the short term, and 'intrinsic' factors as the most enduring and likely to sustain you in developing a career in social work. The overall purpose of CPD is systematic growth. It should form a continuum of learning that is planned and structured, so that its effect is cumulative.

At certain points throughout your career you should stop and reflect on your learning and developmental needs. One such point might be as you approach the end of your first year in practice and move on from NQSW/ASYE status to think about your experiences since qualification and what CPD activity you might not just want to, but have to, engage in, to meet professional, statutory and regulatory requirements.

There may be a number of external factors that will help shape your career development choices. However, it is also important not to forget what you want from your career in social work and where you want to be in the future. There is no single pathway or destination on this journey; each individual is unique. Whilst you may have shared similar experiences with your peers, you will have reached this stage of your career in your own way and only you can decide where you want to go from here.

However, making decisions about your future requires asking questions of yourself and critical reflection on your practice to determine your future CPD plans.

Critical reflection

Critical reflection provides a method by which practitioners can develop their understanding of their CPD needs. Practice is often confused, challenging and complex, and practitioners must frequently rise above the 'routine' to ensure that individuals are supported appropriately. Critical reflection is a theoretical approach and process for analysing and developing practice. It allows the practitioner to explore assumptions and perceptions to challenge preconceived ideas and challenge the status quo. This approach to reflection draws on Schön's (1991) concept of reflecting in and on action, that is during and after the event. However, Schon has been criticised for not including issues of power and politics (Kincheloe 1991) in this model. While self-reflection can be positive for practitioners it is important to remember that critical reflection should include not just a focus on individual practice but also the context in which practice occurs at a structural level (Kam-shing 2006). Otherwise critical reflection runs the risk of becoming destructive for the practitioner if oppressive conditions exist in the practice environment and these are not fully ackowledged. Thomas (2004) suggests that critical reflection needs to move beyond the individual to examine practice in an organisational context; therefore, critical reflection should incorporate practice at an individual and structural level (Askeland 2006).

Critical reflection on action

Critical reflection on action has three key elements:

1. It is retrospective; that is, it occurs after and usually away from the scene of practice.

2. It assumes that practice is underpinned by knowledge.

3. It claims that this knowledge can be increased by a process of analysis and interpretation: the reflective process.

Reflection on action is therefore an active process of transferring experience into knowledge. Reflection should not be confused with thinking about practice, which may only involve recalling what has occurred rather than learning from it. Reflection therefore requires the ability to:

- be self-aware

- describe the experience verbally or in writing

- critically analyse knowledge

- critically analyse feelings

- synthesise new and previous knowledge

- be evaluative, make a judgement about something

- make changes to practice if necessary

- share learning clearly and concisely when appropriate.

Critical reflection in practice is more than just thinking about what has happened in particular case scenarios; it also requires taking action and making changes. The use of the critical incident technique provides one way in which individuals can use critical reflection on practice experience to develop a strategic approach to planning CPD activity.

Critical incident technique

Critical reflection can be used in conjunction with the critical incident technique (Fook and Napier 2000). A critical incident is simply an event which has happened to a practitioner, which they believe is significant in some way (Fook 2003). The 'technique' involves the practitioner analysing an incident, in writing, to discover why they thought it was significant, the context of the incident and what actually happened during the incident.

Fook (2003) suggests the practitioner use the written incident and critical reflection to:

1. identify hidden assumptions

2. examine where the assumptions come from, and how they fit desired theories

3. identify how practice fits with these theories and assumptions.

On answering these questions, practitioners move to Stage 2 to ask:

4. how practice needs to change?

5. what learning is required to facilitate skill enhancement?

6. what type of CPD activity is most appropriate?

Box 8.2 Some questions to aid reflection for developing a personalised approach to CPD

- *The context of CPD:* are you clear why you are participating in it? What is most important to you – is it all about registration or about improving job opportunities or job satisfaction and improved service user outcomes?

- *Lifelong learning:* what type of CPD is required – vocational or educational learning, or both? Can they be combined? How?

- *In what other areas of your life have you engaged in lifelong learning?* How did it feel, what were the costs/benefits to you and those around you, was it worth it? How do you learn? What has worked for you in the past? What has gone wrong in the past? Can you undertake CPD that reflects your learning style to maximise your chances of success?

- *Partnership:* who are your key partners? Are they strong partnerships, do they need improving, what needs to happen to ensure 'good' partnerships?

- *Motivation:* what is your motivation? Is this enough to keep you engaged in CPD activity? What might improve your motivation?

Developing a personalised CPD pathway

Many factors will influence you in determining your CPD path from here; therefore, it is necessary to really think about what *you* want for your future, and what is best for you in the context of your life and those who are part of your life. Again, as discussed in Chapter 5, keeping motivated is going to be crucial to what happens in the future; therefore what you decide to do has to have to be meaningful for you.

Key considerations

- Learning is an activity we all engage in throughout our lives and is part of everyday living.

- As a professional social worker you are expected to continue to engage in learning to further the development of your professional skills. To achieve this you will need to blend both learned and experiential theory and knowledge with practice.

- Engaging in CPD provides a framework and process to facilitate the combining of theory, experience and practice to achieve continued learning.

- CPD should be a continuous process that contributes to your current and future professional and personal developmental needs. Therefore you need to think about, and plan ahead to decide, what type of CPD is most appropriate to help you achieve your goals.

- Practitioners, employers and providers of CPD each have a distinctive role to play in the CPD process.

- At certain points throughout your career you should stop and reflect on your learning and developmental needs.

- Critical reflection is a theoretical approach and process for analysing and developing practice. It allows the practitioner to explore assumptions and perceptions to challenge preconceived ideas and challenge the status quo.

- Many factors will influence you in determining your CPD path from here; therefore it is necessary to really think about what *you* want for your future, and what is best for you in the context of your life, and those who are part of your life.

Conclusion

In this book we have endeavoured to provide some guidance on managing the journey from social work student to NQSW and beyond to professional social work practitioner. Our discussion in Chapter 1 explored some of the thoughts and feelings that might accompany the transition from student to professional, and identified some of the structures designed to support this process. Central to each chapter has been the notion of you as an active pursuer of the relevant skills and knowledge to become not just a capable practitioner but one characterised by professionalism and confidence.

The overarching message of this book is that you should actively seek out, and engage in, the structures and processes that already exist, for example the NQSW framework, to support your transition from student to professional. The NQSW framework has been designed specifically to support you in your development. Whilst the implementation of such a framework may vary from country to country and employer to employer, it is important that right from the start of your career you are proactive in engaging in the development of your skills, knowledge and practice. You should therefore research and understand the purpose and structure of the NQSW framework relevant to you. For example, how is it implemented and what are the respective roles and responsibilities of both you and your employer? Chapter 2 provided a starting point from which to develop your understanding of NQSW status.

As you move into employment as a social worker, a whole new host of challenges may present themselves. Again, there are already structures in place that you can draw on to facilitate a positive experience. The key element in managing this process is preparation. Chapter 3 provided clear guidance on how to prepare yourself for this new challenge, highlighting the fact that starting a new job will always be exciting and challenging. Lessons learnt now and put into practice will therefore be useful throughout your career. Based on research from allied professional groups, this chapter provided a blueprint for starting work in a new organisation/job, one from which you can develop and build your own plan for future career moves.

However, whilst it may seem that much of the transition from student to professional relates to practical issues, some understanding of your professional identity is integral to your development as a professional. This was the focus of Chapter 4. Social work with adults occurs within a variety of professional settings, in both the statutory and non-statutory sectors and alongside a variety of professional groups. It is important for you to develop a clear understanding of different professional roles and a strong sense of your own professional identity in order to know how you fit into the broader context of health and social care settings. Understanding who you are and what makes you different from other professionals is the first step towards developing your professional identity and will provide a foundation on which to build your knowledge and skills and develop your professional practice.

Allied to developing your professional identity is understanding the professional role and tasks. You are entering a profession frequently at the centre of political debate surrounding the role of the state in the lives of individuals and families, where even the status of social work as a 'profession' is challenged. Wider society's understanding of the professional social work role and the tasks you will engage in is often confused, driven as it is by negative media coverage that frequently misrepresents both you and those who access services and leads to unhelpful perceptions and expectations of you as a social work practitioner. Such misconceptions are not new and social work is likely to remain a contentious occupation. However, whilst wider society might not always be clear about what you do, it is important that you have an understanding of what will be expected of you as you enter employment. Chapter 5 provided some guidance on the expectations placed upon the profession and identified the importance of maintaining your motivation to learn and adjust, where necessary, to the changing landscape of professional practice.

Chapter 6 explored supervision. This is one of the larger chapters in the book, which probably reflects its ongoing importance in your professional development. Sadly, supervision can sometimes be viewed as a 'bolt-on' rather than a process central to social work practice. When time and resources are stretched supervision can be viewed almost as an optional extra to practice and professional development. However, nothing could be further from the truth: good supervision, at regular intervals and in its various forms, provides the cornerstone of practice throughout your career and should be an activity you pursue proactively and contribute to.

Even with frameworks, structures, processes and policies designed to support you as a social worker, there is no denying this can be a stressful occupation which can lead to negative feelings that leave you demotivated. Whilst this is to be expected to some extent and for some of the time, given the nature of the types of work undertaken, it is not a given that you will become stressed to such an extent that you 'burn out'. There is a saying: 'forewarned is forearmed'. Chapter 7 provided some of the tools you can use to manage stress and burnout. The key point to remember is that whilst stress and burnout do exist, one does not automatically lead to the other because stress is not inherently bad for you, if managed.

Finally, Chapter 8 provided guidance on planning for your future career. Attaining your social work award was an ending but it also marked a new beginning. The structured nature of your qualifying programme is now absent. Whilst the NQSW framework, induction and supervision provide structures you can use to identify your CPD needs, it will be up to you to ensure you develop the skills and knowledge required to maintain your practice at a level that meets the standards of your employers and the professional regulators. Engagement in CPD activity will provide a pivotal role in your advancement in social work.

Social work as a profession can be stimulating but also frustrating as you attempt to practise in an environment that does not always feel supportive of you or the profession in general. However, within the organisational and structural parameters of health and social care there is still a professional space from which you can develop practice that makes a real difference to those you work with.

Appendix I

NQSW Frameworks Currently in Place in the UK

Here is a brief overview of the current frameworks in place in the UK that might support you in making the transition from student to newly qualified social worker.

England

The NQSW framework in adult and mental health services has developed from the recommendations of the Social Work Task Force (2009), which undertook a comprehensive review of social work in England. In its report *Building a Safe, Confident Future* it identified the first year as a critical time in a social worker's development, and the value of a formal programme of support. This has led to the development of an assessed and supported year in employment as the final stage in becoming a fully fledged social worker, which would serve as a probationary year on completion of the social work degree. The NQSW framework and the ASYE in adult and mental health services is designed specifically to support your transition from social work student to social work practitioner. The framework is not a statutory requirement, so your employer has some flexibility in its application.

To participate in the adult NQSW framework you have to meet four specific criteria: first, to have recently qualified as a social worker; second, be employed, either full- or part-time, in a position working with people who use adult services; third, to be employed in a position which will allow you to meet specific outcome statements contained within the framework; and fourth, to be selected by your employer.

This final point should be clarified by you at the interview stage, as it will give some indication of the level of support you can expect from the prospective employer, because NQSW status has the potential to provide benefits for you. The NQSW framework should give you an opportunity to have an allocated workload proportionate to your level of experience and a commitment from your employer that you receive regular supervision and time for professional development in your first year of practice. You are not formally assessed under the adults framework; however, it does contain 12 outcome statements that NQSWs are expected to evidence in the first year of practice via a portfolio which will be signed off by your supervisor or line manager.

For further information refer to:

> www.skillsforcare.org.uk/socialwork/
> newlyqualifiedsocialworker/NewlyQualifiedSocialWorker.aspx
>
> www.gscc.org.uk

Wales

The Care Council for Wales (CCW), Cyngor Gofal Cymru, is the regulatory body for social work in Wales and it has developed a Continuing Professional Education and Learning framework (CPEL) for social workers.

The structure of the CPEL framework is directly linked to the national career pathway for social workers in Wales (CCW 2011), and it extends beyond the first year in practice, focusing on a longer-term approach. The framework states, 'the role of the NQSW is to continue to meet the requirements of the National Occupational Standards in Social Work and to adhere to the Code of Practice for Social Care Workers' (CCW 2010, p.4). In the first year, in order to make the transition from student to professional, it suggests that you 'will need a well managed and effective period of induction and support' (CCW 2010, p.4). *Making the Most of the First Year in Practice* (CCW 2008a) provides a guide for you on your responsibilities as an NQSW. The guide has been produced in recognition of the importance of your first year in social work practice and its purpose is to support you to:

- make a smooth transition from student to professional practitioner

- consider your responsibilities as an employee

- know what to expect from your employer

- know how you can consolidate and develop social work practice in line with the Care Council's code of practice, CPD and PRTL.

The Care and Social Services Inspectorate Wales (CSSIW) has developed a companion guide for employers entitled *Making the Most of Social Workers' First Year in Practice* (2008). This outlines how government expects employers to support you. Employers are expected to describe:

- the arrangements for supporting and managing you in your first year in practice

- how your first year in practice will be linked to wider strategies for CPD, PRTL and career planning for social work

- what is expected of you.

These two guides overlap to emphasise the joint responsibilities on employers and employees. The guidance indicates what management, support and development you can expect in your first year, and a model to:

- provide you with a mentor who may be the team manager or another designated person

- ensure that you have a personal development plan for your first year of practice that describes the planned opportunities for consolidation and development

- ensure that you have a contractually agreed, protected case- and workload, and time for implementing the development plan

- establish regular supervision that provides reflective learning as well as managing performance

- provide a firm foundation for ongoing development as a professional social worker

- guarantee to service users and carers that you will be supported and managed to be effective.

Although these documents are only for guidance, they do set out a plan of how to meet the code's standards in your first year, and also give you some indication of the type of support you should request of your employer. As an NQSW you will be expected to be following the guide and to have identified, with your employer, consolidation and developmental needs. You will also be expected to meet the code of practice requirements and National Occupational Standards for Social Work, as well as keeping a record of your PRTL for the three-year period of your registration.

For further information refer to:

www.ccwales.org.uk/social-work-students

Northern Ireland

Social work education underwent major reform with the introduction of the new vocational degree in September 2004. At the same time announcements were made regarding the intention to ensure that all new social work graduates undertake an AYE, linked to registration with the Northern Ireland Social Care Council (NISCC). The policy on AYE for new social work graduates was first introduced in 2006 and amended in 2010 following two monitoring reviews which indicated that the AYE was achieving its aim of improving support to new social work graduates, but which also identified some operational difficulties. One significant issue was where social workers might be employed, and whether posts were defined as a suitable for an AYE. Initially it was expected that all NQSW graduates would obtain employment in social work posts; however, the nature of service delivery has changed to such an extent that NQSWs are applying for posts that are not traditional social work posts – for example, the post of project worker within mental health services.

To address this issue, the minimum requirements for AYE registrants are as described below.

- The qualification requirements for the post must include a social work qualification.

- There must be provision for professional supervision by a qualified social worker at least fortnightly for the first six months, and thereafter at least monthly.

- There must be scope within the post for an NQSW to practise the six key social work roles and to consolidate and extend professional skills and knowledge gained on the degree.

- The post should be sufficiently challenging that the NQSW can demonstrate at the end of the year that they are able to practise safely, competently and responsibly as a social worker.

(NISCC 2010, p.6)

You will be required to meet six minimum standards to complete your AYE:

- *Standard 1*: The AYE registrant must have a personal development plan (PDP) which builds on the summary of learning completed at the end of your degree, and opportunities should be made available to meet development needs.

- *Standard 2*: The AYE registrant must receive induction to NISCC induction standards. There should also be induction to the AYE, including information on the employer's systems for support and assessment.

- *Standard 3*: The AYE registrant must have a supervision plan or contract and must receive supervision at least every two weeks during the first six months and thereafter at least monthly, if this is agreed at the interim review (see Standard 5).

- *Standard 4*: The AYE registrant must undertake at least 10 development days as part of the condition of their registration.

- *Standard 5*: There must be an interim review of progress no later than after the first six months. Evidence of reflection on your practice in the six key social work roles should be recorded, and feedback given by your professional supervisor. There should be discussion at this stage about whether the frequency of supervision should be reduced, taking account of the confidence and competence of the AYE registrant and the complexity of the workload.

- *Standard 6*: There should be a final performance appraisal for the AYE year at no later than eleven months. At this stage a decision should be made on whether the AYE registrant is fit to practise as a safe, competent and effective social worker or if an extension is required.

As an NQSW the NISCC identifies seven responsibilities that you must fulfil as an AYE registrant.

1. Apply to the NISCC for registration.

2. Obtain employment in an agency that will provide the opportunity to practise the six key social work roles.

3. Comply and uphold the NISCC code of practice for social care workers.

4. Give your employer your student transcript and personal learning plan, so that your learning in employment can link with their learning as a student.

5. Take responsibility for maintaining and improving your knowledge and skills and recording any professional development activities.

6. Be accountable for the quality of your work and meet relevant standards of practice.

7. Return the signed and endorsed NISCC pro forma confirming successful completion of the AYE, or apply for an extension.

You should expect from your employer as an AYE registrant:

1. Allocation of work that will enable you to engage in the full range of professional social work activity expected of a practising social worker.

2. A formal induction programme.

3. Information from the employer about the standards of practice you are expected to meet, and how your performance will be appraised.

4. Opportunity to meet the NISCC standard of at least 10 developmental days.

5. Access to supervision, support and appraisal, including professional supervision from a registered social worker.

6. An interim review of progress at no later than six months.

7. A final appraisal at no later than 11 months, and signed-off certificate of completion.

The purpose of the certificate of completion is to demonstrate that as an NWSQ you have satisfied your employer that you have met the NISCC AYE standards. It is your responsibility to ensure that this form is completed and returned to the NISCC within one year of you commencing the AYE. Failure to do so may result in your removal from the register, but an extension can be requested if you require more time. The NISCC provides pro formas of all the required documentation, for example the certificate of completion and application for an extension to the AYE.

The AYE process is well established in Northern Ireland, so at interview prospective employers should be able to provide you with clear answers to questions regarding what systems they have in place to support you in meeting AYE requirements. It may also be useful to speak with someone who has already completed their AYE, to try and discover what really happens.

For further information refer to:

www.niscc.info/AssessedYearinEmployment-19.aspx

Scotland

The regulatory body for social work in Scotland is currently the Scottish Social Services Council (SSSC) and the Scottish social services registration rules set down PRTL requirements that all registered newly qualified social workers must meet in order to ensure their continued suitability for registration. The purpose of PRTL is to ensure that as an NQSW you undertake training and learning to assist in consolidating your social work skills, knowledge and values at the outset of your professional career, and to help you contribute to the protection of children and adults.

The registration rules state that:

• Every newly qualified social worker working full time (35 hours a week or more) registered with the Council shall, within the first 12 months of registration, complete 24 days (144 hours) of study, training, courses, seminars, reading, teaching or other activities which could reasonably be expected to advance the social worker's professional development, or contribute to the development of the profession as a whole.

- At least five days (30 hours) must focus on working effectively with colleagues and other professionals to identify, assess and manage risk to vulnerable groups. This is in order to ensure that newly qualified social workers are assisted to meet their primary responsibility of protecting children and vulnerable adults from harm.

- Every social worker registered with the Council shall keep a record of Post Registration Training and Learning undertaken.

- Failure to meet these requirements may be considered misconduct by the Council.

(Scottish Social Services Council 2010)

You will be required to complete a record of achievement to evidence that the training and learning activity undertaken in your workplace within the first year of practice as a social worker meets the PRTL requirements.

Planning your PRTL

Within this framework it is made clear that as an NQSW you have a personal professional responsibility to maintain and develop your social work knowledge, skills and values. It is your responsibility to identify your training and learning needs and look at how these might be met through PRTL. As a graduate of a social work degree the individual learning plan that you completed as part of your course should be the starting point for planning ahead.

A review of PRTL commissioned by the SSSC suggests that approximately 50 per cent of NQSWs were offered induction and support in meeting their PRTL requirements by their employers (Skinner *et al.* 2010). This would seem to suggest that implementation of this framework may vary from employer to employer; therefore, it would be worthwhile at interview stage to ask potential employers what systems they have in place to support you as an NQSW, so as to make a more informed choice (if you have one) if you are offered a job.

For further information refer to:

www.sssc.uk.com/download-document/126

Appendix II

Induction Frameworks and Standards

Refreshed Common Induction Standards (2010) for adult social care in England

Standard 1 – Role of the health and social care worker

Standard 2 – Personal development

Standard 3 – Communicate effectively

Standard 4 – Equality and inclusion

Standard 5 – Principles for implementing duty of care

Standard 6 – Principles of safeguarding in health and social care

Standard 7 – Person-centred support

Standard 8 – Health and safety in an adult social care setting

(Skills for Care 2010a)

Northern Ireland Social Care Council (NISCC) Induction Standards for all new social care workers

Standard 1 – Understand the principles of care

Standard 2 – Understand the organisation and the role of the worker

Standard 3 – Maintain safety at work

Standard 4 – Communicate effectively

Standard 5 – Recognise and respond to abuse and neglect

Standard 6 – Develop as a worker

(Northern Ireland Social Care Council 2007)

Social Care Induction Framework for Wales

Outcome 1 – Understand the principles of care

Outcome 2 – Understand the organisation and the role of the worker

Outcome 3 – Maintain safety at work

Outcome 4 – Communicate effectively

Outcome 5 – Recognise and respond to abuse and neglect

Outcome 6 – Develop as a worker

(Care Council for Wales 2008b)

Preparing for Practice – Induction Guidance for Social Services Employers in Scotland

- Values
- Introduction to social service practice
- Introduction to organisation
- Service specific
- The workplace

(Scottish Social Services Council 2011)

Appendix III

Legislation, Policy and National Practice Guidance: Some Key Examples

Client group/ setting	Key legislation/policy	Details
General – adult settings	*A Vision for Adult Social Care: Capable Communities and Active Citizens* (Department of Health 2010a)	Principles for adult social care and future reform, e.g. personalised services
	Health Act 2009	NHS care and services
	Personal Health Budgets: First Steps (Department of Health 2009b)	Personal budgets
	Health and Social Care Act 2008	Modernisation and integration of health and social care Care Quality Commission Registration and inspection of providers
	Putting People First: A Shared Vision and Commitment to the Transformation of Adult Social Care (Department of Health 2007b)	Shared aims and values that guide the transformation
	Mental Capacity Act 2005	Statutory framework for people who lack capacity to make decisions about treatment and care Capacity test, best interests checklist, advance decisions, Court of Protection, independent mental capacity advocates (IMCAs)
	National Health Service Act 2006	Non-residential services in respect of illness
	Carers (Equal Opportunities) Act 2004	Duties on local authorities to inform carers of rights to assessment

	Community Care (Delayed Discharges) Act 2003	Communication between health and social care systems
	Health and Social Care Act 2001	Extending rights to choose and pay own service provider
	Carers and Disabled Children Act 2000	Carers' assessment and services
	No Secrets (Department of Health and Home Office 2000)	Adult protection
	Care Standards Act 2000	Protection of vulnerable adults (POVA)
	Human Rights Act 1998	Requirements on public authorities
	Housing Act 1996	Allocating/priority of housing
	Disability Discrimination Act 1995	Section 21: implications for health service provision
	Community Care (Direct Payments) Act 1996	Rights to choose and pay own service provider
	Carers (Recognition and Services) Act 1995	Carers' assessments
	NHS and Community Care Act 1990	Community care assessments, duties to assess and provide care
	Children Act 1989	Supporting families and children in need
	Chronically Sick and Disabled Persons Act 1970	Non-residential welfare services for disabled people
	National Assistance Act 1948	Residential accommodation Non-residential welfare services Removal of vulnerable groups from home Protection of property
Mental health	Living Well with Dementia – A National Strategy (Department of Health 2009a)	Dementia services
	Refocusing the Care Programme Approach: Policy and Positive Practice Guidance (Department of Health 2008b) CPA first introduced in HC (90)23/ LASSL (90)11 Joint Health and Social Services Circular (Department of Health 1990)	Changes to Care Programme Approach – a framework for the assessment, care planning, care coordination and review of people with severe mental illness
	Code of Practice: Mental Health Act 1983 (2008)	Amended code of practice

	Mental Health Act 1983 (amended 2007)	Powers to detain and treat people with a mental disorder Consent to treatment provisions Tribunals Community provisions, police powers
	National Service Framework (Department of Health 1999) *National Service Framework for Mental Health – Five Years on* (Appleby 2004)	Standards in mental health
	The Ten Essential Capabilities – A Framework for the Whole of the Mental Health Workforce (Hope 2004)	Identified the essential capabilities that need to be achieved in the education and training of mental health workers
Learning Disability	*Valuing People* (Cm 5086 2001)	First White Paper on learning disability for 30 years, highlighting principles of civil rights, independence, choice and inclusion
	Valuing People Now: A New Three-Year Strategy for People with Learning Disabilities (Department of Health 2009c)	Sets out the government strategy for people with learning disabilities, including greater choice and control for them, and person-centred plans
	Independence, Choice and Risk: A Guide to Best Practice in Supported Decision-making (Department of Health 2007a)	Best practice guide for all health and social care practitioners working with adults
Older persons	*National Service Framework for Older People* (Department of Health 2001)	Removal of discrimination in the provision of services on account of age
	Health Services and Public Health Act 1968	Non-residential services for older people

References

American Psychiatric Association (APA) (2001) *Diagnostic and Statistical Manual of Mental Disorders, Fourth Edition, Text Revision (DSM-IV-TR)*. Washington, DC: APA.

Appleby, L. (2004) *The National Service Framework for Mental Health – Five Years On*. London: Department of Health. Available at www.dh.gov.uk/en/Publicationsandstatistics/Publications/PublicationsPolicyAndGuidance/DH_4099120, accessed on 17 August 2011.

Askeland, A. G. (2006) 'Linking critical reflection and qualitative research.' *International Social Work 49*, 6, 731–743.

Banks, S. (2006) *Ethics and Values in Social Work*, 3rd edn. Basingstoke: Palgrave Macmillan.

Banks, S. (2009) 'Professional Values and Accountability.' In R. Adams, L. Dominelli and M. Payne (eds) *Critical Practice in Social Work*. Basingstoke: Palgrave Macmillan.

Bates, N., Immins, T., Parker, J., Keen, S. *et al.* (2010) 'Baptism of fire: The first year in the life of a newly qualified social worker.' *Social Work Education 29*, 2, 152–170.

Beckett, C. and Maynard, A. (2005) *Values and Ethics in Social Work: An Introduction*. London: Sage Publications.

Beddoe, L. (2010) 'Surveillance or reflection: Professional supervision in "the risk society".' *British Journal of Social Work 40*, 4, 1279–1296.

Biesteck, F. (1961) *The Casework Relationship*. London: George Allen and Unwin.

Blair, S.E.E. (2000) 'The centrality of occupation during life transitions.' *British Journal of Occupational Therapy 63*, 5, 231–237.

Boshuizen, H., Rainer, B. and Gruber, H. (2004) *Professional Learning: Gaps and Transitions on the Way from Novice to Expert*. Berlin: Kluwer Academic Publishers.

Bradley, G. (2006) 'Using research findings to change agency culture and practice.' *Research, Policy and Planning 24*, 3, 135–148.

Bridges, W. (1998) 'Managing transitions: Making the most of change.' *Personnel Review 24*, 2, 135–148.

British Association of Social Workers (BASW) (2002) *The Code of Ethics for Social Work*. Birmingham: BASW. Available at www.basw.co.uk/about/code-of-ethics, accessed on 19 August 2011.

Brown, A. and Bourne, I. (1996) *The Social Work Supervisor*. Buckingham: Open University Press.

Cameron, C. (2003) 'Care Work and Care Workers.' In *Social Care Workforce Research: Needs and Priorities. Final Report of the Expert Seminar 15th and 16th May 2003*. London: Social Care Workforce Research Unit, Kings College London.

Care and Social Services Inspectorate Wales (CSSIW) (2008) *Making the Most of Social Workers' First Year in Practice*. Cardiff: Care and Social Services Inspectorate Wales. Available at http://wales.gov.uk/cssiwsubsite/newcssiw/publications/ourfindings/allwales/2008/1styear/?lang=en, accessed on 24 August 2011.

Care Council for Wales (CCW) (2008a) *Making the Most of the First Year in Practice: A Guide for Newly Qualified Social Workers*. Cardiff: Care Council for Wales. Available at www.ccwales.org.uk/qualifications-and-careers/qualifications/post-qualifying, accessed on 24 August 2011.

Care Council for Wales (CCW) (2008b) *Social Care Induction Framework for Wales*. Cardiff: Care Council for Wales. Available at www.ccwales.org.uk/qualifications-and-careers/qualifications/induction-framework, accessed on 24 August 2011.

Care Council for Wales (CCW) (2010) *Code of Practice for Social Care Workers*. Cardiff: Care Council for Wales. Available at www.ccwales.org.uk/registration-and-conduct/confidence-in-care/the-codes-of-practice, accessed on 16 August 2011.

Care Council for Wales (CCW) (2011) *Continuing Professional Education and Learning: A Framework for Social Workers in Wales. Consultation Document June–September 2011*. Cardiff: Care Council for Wales.

Carver, C., Scheier, M. and Weintraub, J. (1989) 'Assessing coping strategies: A theoretically based approach.' *Journal of Personality and Social Psychology 56*, 2, 267–283.

Cassedy, P., Epling, M., Williamson, L. and Harvey, G. (2001) 'Providing Cross Discipline Supervision to New Supervisors.' In J. Cutliffe, T. Butterworth and B. Proctor (eds) *Clinical Supervision*. London: Routledge.

Central Council for Education and Training in Social Work (CCETSW) (1998) *Post Qualifying Education and Training: The Accreditation Handbook*. London: CCETSW.

Chang, E. and Hancock, K. (2003) 'Role stress and role ambiguity in new nursing graduates in Australia.' *Nursing and Health Sciences 5*, 2, 155–163.

Chickering, A.W. and Reisser, L. (1993) *Education and Identity*, 2nd edn. San Fransisco: Jossey-Bass.

Cm 5086 (2001) *Valuing People: A New Strategy for Learning Disability for the 21st Century – a White Paper*. London: The Stationery Office. Available at www.dh.gov.uk/en/Publicationsandstatistics/Publications/PublicationsPolicyAndGuidance/DH_4009153, accessed on 18 August 2011.

Collins, S. (2008) 'Statutory social workers: Stress, job satisfaction, coping, social support and individual differences.' *British Journal of Social Work 38*, 6, 1173–1193.

Commission for Healthcare Audit and Inspection (2007) *Investigation into the Service for People with Learning Disabilities provided by Sutton and Merton Primary Care Trust*. London: Healthcare Commission. Available at www.cqc.org.uk/publications.cfm?widCall1=customDocManager.search_do_2&tcl_id=2&top_parent=4513&tax_child=4574&tax_grand_child=4575&tax_great_grand_child=4601&search_string=, accessed on 23 August 2011.

Community Care (2010a) '40% of newly qualified staff slam £5m support scheme.' *Community Care*, 23 November. Available at www.communitycare.co.uk/Articles/2010/11/23/115867/40-of-newly-qualified-staff-slam-5m-support-scheme.htm, accessed on 24 August 2011.

Community Care (2010b) 'Working lives: How to be resilient in the workplace.' *Community Care*, 7 May. Available at www.communitycare.co.uk/Articles/2010/05/07/114446/working-lives-how-to-be-resilient-in-the-workplace.htm, accessed on 24 August 2011.

Cooper, B. (2008) 'Continuing Professional Development: A Critical Approach.' In S. Fraser and S. Matthews (eds) *The Critical Practitioner in Health and Social Care*. Milton Keynes: Open University and Sage.

Cooper, C. L. and Rousseau, D.M. (2001) Employee Versus Owner Issues in Organisations. *Trends in Organisational Behaviour*, Volume 8. New York: Wiley.

Cornwall Adult Protection Committee (2007) *The Murder of Steven Hoskin: Serious Case Review. Multi-agency and Single-agency Recommendations and Action Plans*. Available at www.cornwall.gov.uk/default.aspx?page=5609, accessed on 17 August 2011.

Cornwall and Isles of Scilly Safeguarding Adults Board (2009) *Serious Case Review. Executive Summary Report of a Female Adult (JK)*. Cornwall and Isles of Scilly Safeguarding Adults Board.

Cree, V. and Wallace, S. (2009) 'Risk and Protection.' In R. Adams, L. Dominelli and M. Payne (2009) (eds) *Practising Social Work in a Complex World*. Basingstoke: Palgrave Macmillan.

Davis, M.H. (1983) 'Measuring individual differences in empathy.' *Journal of Personality and Social Psychology 44*, 1, 113–126.

Davys, A. and Beddoe, L. (2010) *Best Practice in Professional Supervision. A Guide for the Helping Professions*. London: Jessica Kingsley Publishers.

Delaney, C. (2003) 'Walking a fine line: Graduate nurses' transition experiences during orientation.' *Journal of Nursing Education 42*, 10, 437–443.

Delors, J., Al Mufti, I., Amagi, I., Carneiro, R. *et al.* (1996) *Learning: The Treasure Within: Report to UNESCO of the International Commission on Education for the Twenty-first Century*. Paris: UNESCO Publishing. Available at www.see-educoop.net/education_in/pdf/15_62.pdf, accessed on 24 August 2011.

Department of Health (1990) Joint Health and Social Services Circular HC(90)23/LASSL(90)11 *The Care Programme Approach for People with a Mental Illness, Referred to Specialist Psychiatric Services*. London: Department of Health.

Department of Health (1999) *National Service Framework for Mental Health: Modern Standards and Service Models*. London: Department of Health.

Department of Health (2001) *National Service Framework for Older People*. London: Department of Health. Available at www.dh.gov.uk/en/Publicationsandstatistics/Publications/PublicationsPolicyAndGuidance/DH_4003066, accessed on 17 August 2011.

Department of Health (2007a) *Independence, Choice and Risk: A Guide to Best Practice in Supported Decision Making*. London: Department of Health. Available at www.dh.gov.uk/en/Publicationsandstatistics/Publications/PublicationsPolicyAndGuidance/DH_074773, accessed on 17 August 2011.

Department of Health (2007b) *Putting People First: A Shared Vision and Commitment to the Transformation of Adult Social Care.* Available at www.dh.gov.uk/en/Publicationsandstatistics/Publications/PublicationsPolicyAndGuidance/DH_081118, accessed on 17 August 2011.

Department of Health (2008a) *Code of Practice: Mental Health Act 1983.* London: The Stationery Office. Available at www.dh.gov.uk/en/Publicationsandstatistics/Publications/PublicationsPolicyAndGuidance/DH_084597, accessed on 17 August 2011.

Department of Health (2008b) *Refocusing the Care Programme Approach: Policy and Positive Practice Guidance* London: Department of Health. Available at www.dh.gov.uk/en/Publicationsandstatistics/Publications/PublicationsPolicyAndGuidance/DH_083647, accessed on 17 August 2011.

Department of Health (2009a) *Living Well with Dementia: A National Strategy.* London: Department of Health. Available at www.dh.gov.uk/en/Publicationsandstatistics/Publications/PublicationsPolicyAndGuidance/DH_094058, accessed on 17 August 2011.

Department of Health (2009b) *Personal Health Budgets: First Steps.* London: Department of Health. Available at www.dh.gov.uk/en/Publicationsandstatistics/Publications/PublicationsPolicyAndGuidance/DH_093842, accessed on 17 August 2011.

Department of Health (2009c) *Valuing People Now: A New Three-Year Strategy for People with Learning Disabilities.* London: Department of Health. Available at www.dh.gov.uk/en/Publicationsandstatistics/Publications/PublicationsPolicyAndGuidance/DH_093377, accessed on 15 August 2011.

Department of Health (2010a) *A Vision for Adult Social Care: Capable Communities and Active Citizens.* London: Department of Health. Available at www.dh.gov.uk/en/Publicationsandstatistics/Publications/PublicationsPolicyAndGuidance/DH_121508, accessed on 17 August 2011.

Department of Health (2010b) *Prioritising Need in the Context of Putting People First: A Whole System Approach to Eligibility for Social Care, England 2010.* London: Department of Health. Available at www.dh.gov.uk/en/Publicationsandstatistics/Publications/PublicationsPolicyAndGuidance/DH_113154, accessed on 16 August 2011.

Department of Health, Association of Directors of Adult Social Services (ADASS), Skills for Care, BASW and the Social Care Association (2010) *The Future of Social Work in Adult Social Services in England.* Available at www.dh.gov.uk/en/Publicationsandstatistics/Publications/PublicationsPolicyAndGuidance/DH_114571, accessed on 12 August 2011.

Department of Health and Home Office (2000) *No Secrets: Guidance on Developing and Implementing Multi-agency Policies and Procedures to Protect Vulnerable Adults from Abuse.* London: Department of Health. Available at www.dh.gov.uk/en/Publicationsandstatistics/Publications/PublicationsPolicyAndGuidance/DH_4008486, accessed on 16 August 2011.

Dickens, J. (2009) *Social Work and Social Policy: An Introduction.* London: Routledge.

Dolan, P., Hallsworth, M., Halpern, D., King, D. and Vlaev I. (2010) *Mindspace: Influencing Behaviour through Public Policy.* London: Institute for Government. Available at www.instituteforgovernment.org.uk/images/files/MINDSPACE-full.pdf, accessed on 24 August 2011.

Donnellan, H. and Jack, G. (2010) *The Survival Guide for Newly Qualified Child and Family Social Workers*. London: Jessica Kingsley Publishers.

Dreyfus, H. and Dreyfus, S. (1986) *Mind Over Machine. The Power of Human Intuition and Expertise in the Era of the Computer*. Oxford: Basil Blackwell.

East London NHS Foundation Trust (2009) *Independent Inquiry into the Care and Treatment of Peter Bryan. Part One* and *Part Two*. London: NHS London. Available at www.london.nhs.uk/publications/independent-publications/independent-inquiries/independent-reports-published-into-care-and-treatment-of-pb, accessed on 23 August 2011.

Engel, G.V. (1970) 'Professional autonomy and bureacratic organization.' *Administrative Science Quarterly 15*, 1, 12–21.

Eraut, M. (1994) *Developing Professional Knowledge and Competence*. London: Falmer.

Fenge, L. (2009) 'Managing Transitions.' In S. Keen, I. Gray, J. Parker, D. Galpin and K. Brown (2009) (eds) *Newly Qualified Social Workers: A Handbook for Practice*. Exeter: Learning Matters.

Ferguson, I. and Woodward, R. (2009) *Radical Social Work Practice*. Bristol: Policy Press.

Field, J. (2008) 'Rethinking supervision and shaping future practice.' *Social Work Now 40*, August, 11–18.

Fook, J. (2003) *Social Work: Critical Theory and Practice*. London: Sage.

Fook, J. and Napier, L. (2000) *Breakthroughs in Practice: Theorising Critical Moments in Social Work*. London: Whiting & Birch.

Fouad, N.A. and Bynner, J. (2008) 'Work transitions.' *American Psychologist 63*, 4, 241–251.

Freudenberger, H. and Richelson, G. (1980) *Burnout: The High Cost of High Achievement. What It Is and How to Survive It*. New York: Bantam Books.

Friborg, O., Hjemdal, O., Rosenvinge, J.H. and Martinussen, M. (2003) 'A new rating scale for adult resilience: What are the central protective resources behind healthy adjustment?' *International Journal of Methods in Psychiatric Research 12*, 2, 65–76.

Galpin, D. (2009) 'Who really drives the development of post-qualifying social work education and what are the implications of this?' *Social Work Education 28*, 1, 65–80.

General Social Care Council (GSCC) (2004, updated 2010) *Code of Practice for Social Care Workers and Code of Practice for Employers of Social Care Workers*. London: General Social Care Council. Available at www.gscc.org.uk/codes, accessed on 19 August 2011.

General Social Care Council (GSCC) (2008) *A Statement of Social Work Roles and Tasks for the 21st Century*. London: General Social Care Council. Available at www.gscc.org.uk/cmsFiles/Policy/Roles%20and%20Tasks.PDF, accessed on 24 August 2011.

Gerrish, K. (2001) 'Still fumbling along? A comparative study of the newly qualified nurse's perception of the transition from student to qualified nurse.' *Journal of Advanced Nursing 32*, 2, 473–480.

Gibb, M. (2009) 'Report warns over social services.' *BBC News*, 28 July 2009. Available at http://news.bbc.co.uk/1/hi/uk/8173443.stm, accessed on 26 September 2011.

Gibb, M. (2010) 'Letter to ministers on behalf of the Social Work Reform Board, 17 August 2010.' Available at www.socialworkconnections.org.uk/docs/TimLoughton.pdf, accessed on 16 August 2011.

Gilbert, T. (2001) 'Reflective practice and clinical supervision: Meticulous rituals of the confessional.' *Journal of Advanced Nursing 36*, 2, 199–205.

Gilligan, R. (1997) 'Beyond permanence? The importance of resilience in child placement practice and planning.' *Adoption and Fostering 21*, 1, 12–20.

Goleman, D. (1996) *Emotional Intelligence. Why It Can Matter More than IQ.* London: Bloomsbury.

Golightley, M. (2008) *Social Work and Mental Health*, 3rd edn. Exeter: Learning Matters.

Grace, A. P. (2004) 'Lifelong learning as a chameleonic concept and versatile practice: Y2K perspectives and trends.' *International Journal of Lifelong Education 23*, 4, 385–405.

Gray, I. (2009) 'Managing Induction, Probation and Supervision.' In S. Keen, I. Gray, J. Parker, D. Galpin and K. Brown (2009) (eds) *Newly Qualified Social Workers: A Handbook for Practice.* Exeter: Learning Matters

Greenwood, E. (1957) 'Attributes of a profession.' *Social Work 2*, 3, 45–55.

Hafford-Letchfield, T. (2006) *Management and Organisations in Social Work.* Exeter: Learning Matters.

Hafford-Letchfield, T., Leonard, K., Begum, N. and Chick, N. (2008) *Leadership and Management in Social Care.* London: Sage Publications.

Haringey Local Safeguarding Children Board (2009) *Serious Case Review 'Child A'.* London: Department for Education. Available at www.education.gov.uk/inthenews/inthenews/a0065565/peter-connelly-serious-case-review-reports-published, accessed on 23 August 2011.

Hawkins, P. and Shohet, R. (2006) *Supervision in the Helping Professions*, 3rd edn. Maidenhead: Open University Press McGraw Hill.

Health and Safety Executive (2011) 'What is stress?' Available at www.hse.gov.uk/stress/furtheradvice/whatisstress.htm, accessed on 24 August 2011.

Herald, J. and Lymbery, M. (2002) 'The social work role in multi-disciplinary teams.' *Practice 14*, 4, 17–27.

Herzberg, F. (1972) 'One More Time: How Do You Motivate Employees?' In L. Davis and J. Taylor *Design of Jobs.* London: Penguin.

Honey, P. and Mumford, A. (1986) *Using Your Learning Styles.* Maidenhead: Peter Honey Publications.

Hope, R. (2004) *The Ten Essential Shared Capabilities – A Framework for the Whole of the Mental Health Workforce.* London: Department of Health. Available at www.dh.gov.uk/en/Publicationsandstatistics/Publications/PublicationsPolicyAndGuidance/DH_4087169, accessed on 17 August 2011.

Horner, L. and Jones, A. (2004) *Living on the Frontline: A Future for the Civil Service.* London: The Work Foundation. Available at www.theworkfoundation.com/research/publications/publicationdetail.aspx?oItemId=165&parentPageID=102&PubType=, accessed on 24 August 2011.

Howard, F. (2008) 'Managing stress or enhancing wellbeing? Positive psychology's contributions to clinical supervision.' *Australian Psychologist 43*, 2, 105–113. Available at www.clinica.divisionescolpsic.org/articulos-docs/Managing_stress_enhancing.pdf, accessed on 24 August 2011.

Howe, K. (2009) 'Managing the Personal: From Surviving to Thriving in Social Work.' In S. Keen, I. Gray, J. Parker, D. Galpin and K. Brown (eds) *Newly Qualified Social Workers: A Handbook for Practice.* Exeter: Learning Matters.

Hughes, L. and Pengelly, P. (1997) *Staff Supervision in a Turbulent Environment: Managing Process and Task in Front-line Services.* London: Jessica Kingsley Publishers.

Huxley, P., Evans, S., Gately, C., Webber, M. *et al.* (2005) 'Stress and pressures in mental health social work: The worker speaks.' *British Journal of Social Work 35,* 1063–1079.

Inskipp, F. and Proctor, B. (1993) *Making the Most of Supervision. A Professional Development Resource for Counsellors, Supervisors and Trainers.* Twickenham: Cascade.

International Federation of Social Work (IFSW) (2000) 'Definition of social work.' Available at www.ifsw.org/f38000138.html, accessed on 2 February 2011.

Johns, C. (2001) 'Depending on the intent and the emphasis of the supervisor, clinical supervision can be a different experience.' *Journal of Nursing Management 9,* 3, 139–145.

Johnson, K. and Williams, I. (2007) *Managing Uncertainty and Change in Social Work and Social Care.* Lyme Regis: Russell House Publishing.

Jones, C. (2001) 'Voices from the front line: State social workers and New Labour.' *British Journal of Social Work 31,* 4, 547–562.

Kadushin, A. (1976) *Supervision in Social Work.* New York: Columbia University Press.

Kadushin, A. (1992) *Supervision in Social Work,* 3rd edn. New York: Columbia University Press.

Kam-shing, Y. (2006) 'Self-reflection in reflective practice: A note of caution.' *British Journal of Social Work 36,* 5, 777–788.

Keen, S., Gray, I., Parker, J., Galpin, D. and Brown, K. (2009) *Newly Qualified Social Workers: A Handbook for Practice.* Exeter: Learning Matters.

Kincheloe, J. L. (1991) *Teachers as Researchers: Qualitative Inquiry as a Path to Empowerment.* London: Falmer Press.

Kinman, G. and Grant, L. (2010) *Emotional Intelligence, Reflective Abilities and Wellbeing in Social Workers and Related Skills in Predicting Wellbeing and Performance in Social Work Practice.* Luton: Centre for Excellence in Teaching and Learning. Available at www.beds.ac.uk/bridgescetl/out/reports/emotionalintelligence, accessed on 24 August 2011.

Koerin, B., Harrigan, M. and Reeves, J. (1990) 'Facilitating the transition from student to social worker: Challenges of the younger student.' *Journal of Social Work Education 26,* 2, 199–207.

Kolb, D. (1984) *Experiential Learning as the Source of Learning and Development.* New York: Prentice Hall.

Kramer, M. (1974) *Reality Shock: Why Nurses Leave Nursing.* St Louis, Mo: C.V. Mosby.

Lacey, C. (1977) *The Socialisation of Teachers.* London: Methuen.

Laming (2003) *The Victoria Climbié Inquiry. Report of an Inquiry by Lord Laming.* London: The Stationery Office. Available at www.dh.gov.uk/en/Publicationsandstatistics/Publications/PublicationsPolicyAndGuidance/DH_4008654, accessed on 17 August 2011.

Laming (2009) *The Protection of Children in England: A Progress Report.* London: The Stationery Office. Available at www.education.gov.uk/publications/standard/publicationdetail/page1/HC%20330, accessed on 19 August 2011.

Lazarus, R. (1998) *The Life and Work of an Eminent Psychologist: Autobiography of Richard S. Lazarus.* New York: Springer.

Maslow, A.H. (1943) 'A theory of human motivation.' *Psychological Review 50*, 370–396.

McClelland, D.C., Atkinson, J.W., Clark, R.A. and Lowell E.L. (1953) *The Achievement Motive.* Princeton, NJ: Van Nostrand.

McGregor, D. (1960) *The Human Side of Enterprise.* New York: McGraw-Hill.

Ministry of Justice (2008) *Mental Capacity Act 2005: Deprivation of Liberty Safeguards – Code of Practice to Supplement the Main Mental Capacity Act 2005 Code of Practice.* London: The Stationery Office. Available at www.dh.gov.uk/en/Publicationsandstatistics/Publications/PublicationsPolicyAndGuidance/DH_085476, accessed on 19 August 2011.

Molasso, W.R. (2006) 'Measuring a student's sense of purpose in life.' *Michigan Journal of College Student Development 12*, 1, 15–24.

Morrison, T. (2005) *Staff Supervision in Social Care: Making a Real Difference for Staff and Service Users,* 3rd edn. Brighton: Pavilion.

Morrison, T. (2007) 'Emotional intelligence, emotion and social work: Context, characteristics, complications and contribution.' *British Journal of Social Work 37*, 2, 245–263.

Newton, J. and McKenna, L. (2006) 'The transitional journey through the graduate year: A focus group study.' *International Journal of Nursing Studies 44*, 7, 1231–1237.

NHS London (2010) 'Findings of reviews into care and treatment of 21 mental health patients – February 2010.' Available at www.london.nhs.uk/publications/independent-publications/independent-inquiries/findings-of-reviews-into-care-and-treatment-of-21-mental-health-patients--february-2010, accessed on 17 August 2011.

Northern Ireland Social Care Council (NISCC) (2007) *Induction Standards NI: Standards for New Workers in Social Care.* Belfast: NISCC. Available at www.niscc.info/InductionStandards-109.aspx, accessed on 19 August 2011.

Northern Ireland Social Care Council (NISCC) (2010) *The Assessed Year in Employment (AYE) for Newly Qualified Social Workers in NI. Revised Guidance for Registrants and their Employers.* Belfast: NISCC. Available at www.niscc.info/2010-321.aspx, accessed on 17 August 2011.

Odro, A., Vlancy, C. and Foster, J. (2010) 'Bridging the theory–practice gap in student nurse training: An evaluation of a personal and professional development programme.' *The Journal of Mental Health Training, Education and Practice 5*, 2, 4–12.

Oko, J. (2009) *Understanding and Using Theory in Social Work.* Exeter: Learning Matters.

Organisation of Economic Co-operation and Development (OECD) (2007) 'Qualifications and lifelong learning. Policy Brief.' Paris: OECD. Available from www.oecd.org/dataoecd/10/2/38500491.pdf, accessed on 10 December 2010.

Parker, J. and Whitfield, J. (2006) *Effective Practice Learning in Local Authorities (2). Workforce Development, Recruitment and Retention.* Leeds: Practice Learning Taskforce. Available at www.skillsforcare.org.uk/nmsruntime/saveasdialog.aspx?lID=1104&sID=1377, accessed on 24 August 2011.

Parrott, L. (2006) *Values and Ethics in Social Work.* Exeter: Learning Matters.

Pawson, R., Boaz, A., Grayson, L., Long, A. and Barnes, C. (2003) *Types and Quality of Knowledge in Social Care.* Knowledge Review 3. London: Social Care Institute for Excellence. Available at www.scie.org.uk/publications/knowledgereviews/kr03.asp, accessed on 24 August 2011.

Peach, J. and Horner, N. (2007) 'Using Supervision: Support or Surveillance.' In M. Lymbery and K. Postle (eds) *Social Work: A Companion to Learning.* London: Sage.

Pearson, G. (1973) 'Social work as the privatised solution of public ills.' *British Journal of Social Work 3,* 2, 209–227.

Pettes, D. (1967) *Supervision in Social Work.* New York: Columbia University Press.

Pietroni, P. (1991) 'Stereotypes or archetypes? A study of perceptions amongst health care students.' *Journal of Social Work Practice 5,* 1, 61–69.

Platt, D. (2003) *Modern Social Services: A Commitment to the Future – 12th Annual Report of the Chief Inspector of Social Services 2002–2003.* London: Department of Health.

Prince, K., Van de Wiel, M., Van der Vleuten, C., Boshuizen, H. and Scherpbier, A. (2004) 'Junior doctors' opinions about the transition from medical school to clinical practice: A change of environment.' *Education for Health 17,* 3, 323–331. Available at www.educationforhealth.net/EfHArticleArchive/1357-6283_v17n3s7_713994292.pdf, accessed on 24 August 2011.

Reynolds, J. (2007) 'Discourses of inter-professionalism.' *British Journal of Social Work 37,* 3, 441–457.

Ritchie, J., Dick, D. and Lingham, R. (1994) *The Report of the Inquiry into the Care and Treatment of Christopher Clunis.* London: HMSO.

Rogers, J. (1993) *Adults Learning,* 4th edn. Buckingham: Open University Press.

Rolfe, G., Freshwater, D. and Jasper, M. (2001) *Critical Reflection in Nursing and the Helping Professions: A User's Guide.* Basingstoke: Palgrave Macmillan.

Rönkä, A., Oravala, S. and Pulkkinen, L. (2003) 'Turning points in adults' lives: The effects of gender and the amount of choice.' *Journal of Adult Development 10,* 3, 203–215.

Ryan, T. and Pritchard, J. (2004) *Good Practice in Adult Mental Health.* London: Jessica Kingsley Publishers.

Scottish Executive Education Department (2005) *Insight 25: The Role of the Social Worker in the 21st Century – A Literature Review.* Edinburgh: Scottish Executive Education Department. Available at http://scotland.gov.uk/Publications/2005/12/1394855/48583, accessed on 17 August 2011.

Scottish Social Services Council (SSSC) (2010) *Post Registration Training and Learning: Requirements for Newly Qualified Social Workers (NQSWs). Guidance Notes for NQSWs.* Dundee: Scottish Social Services Council. Available at www.sssc.uk.com/component/option,com_docman/Itemid,486/gid,190/task,cat_view, accessed on 16 August 2011.

Scottish Social Services Council (SSSC) (2011) *Preparing for Practice – Induction Guidance for Social Service Employers in Scotland.* Dundee: Scottish Social Services Council. Available at www.sssc.uk.com/preparingforpractice, accessed on 17 August 2011.

Schön, D. (1987) *Educating the Reflective Practitioner.* San Fransisco: Jossey-Bass.

Schön, D. (1991) *The Reflective Practitioner: How Professionals Think in Action.* Avebury: Ashgate Publishing.

Schrader, A. (2008) 'Hitchhiking across cultures from the classroom to the workplace.' *Feliciter 54*, 2, 43–44.

Seebohm, F. (1968) *Report of the Committee on Local Authority and Allied Personal Social Services.* London: HMSO.

Shardlow, S. (1998) 'Values, Ethics and Social Work.' In R. Adams, L. Dominelli and M. Payne (eds) *Social Work Themes, Issues and Critical Debates.* Basingstoke: Macmillan.

Shulman, L. (1999) *The Skills of Helping Individuals, Families, Groups and Communities*, 4th edn. Ithaca, Ill.: Peacock Publishers.

Skills for Care (2004) *Social Work National Occupational Standards (NOS).* Available at www.skillsforcare.org.uk/developing_skills/National_Occupational_Standards/social_work_NOS.aspx, accessed on 16 August 2011.

Skills for Care (2010a) *Common Induction Standards (2010 'refreshed' edition) Social Care (Adults, England) with Glossary.* Leeds: Skills for Care. Available at www.skillsforcare.org.uk/cis, accessed on 17 August 2011.

Skills for Care (2010b) *Keeping up the Good Work – A Practical Guide to Implementing Continuing Professional Development in the Adult Social Care Workforce.* Leeds: Skills for Care. Available at www.skillsforcare.org.uk/developing_skills/CPD_and_careerpathways/cpd.aspx, accessed on 22 August 2011.

Skills for Care (2011) *Getting a good start. Evaluation of the first year of the Newly Qualified Social Worker Framework for adult service 2009/10.* Leeds: Skills for Care.

Skinner, K., Macrae, R., Henery N. and Snowball, A. (2010) *Evaluation of the Post Registration Training and Learning of Newly Qualified Social Workers.* Dundee: Scottish Social Services Council. Available at www.sssc.uk.com, accessed on 16 August 2011.

Social Work Reform Board (2010) *Building a Safe, Confident Future, One Year On.* London: SWRB.

Social Work Reform Board (2011) *Professional Standards for Social Workers in England.* London: SWRB. Available at www.education.gov.uk/swrb/a0074240/professional-standards-for-social-workers-in-england, accessed on 27 September 2011.

Social Work Task Force (SWTF) (2009) *Building a Safe, Confident Future. The Final Report of the Social Work Task Force: November 2009.* London: DCSF. Available at www2.warwick.ac.uk/fac/soc/shss/courses/social_work_task_force_final_report.pdf, accessed on 24 August 2011.

South West London Strategic Health Authority (2006) *The Independent Inquiry into the Care and Treatment of John Barrett.* London: NHS London. Available at www.london.nhs.uk/publications/independent-inquiries/john-barrett-report, accessed on 23 August 2011.

Stalker, C.A., Mandell, D., Frensch, K.M., Harvey, C. and Wright, M. (2007) 'Child welfare workers who are exhausted yet satisfied with their jobs. How do they do it?' *Child and Family Social Work 12*, 2, 182–191.

Thomas, N.K. (2004) 'Resident burnout.' *Journal of the American Medical Association 292*, 23, 2880–2889.

Thompson, N. (2006) *Anti-discriminatory Practice*, 4th edn. London: Palgrave Macmillan.

Trevithick, P. (2003) 'Effective relationship-based practice: A theoretical explanation.' *Journal of Social Work Practice 17*, 2, 163–176.

Tsui, M. (2005) *Social Work Supervision: Contexts and Concepts*. Thousand Oaks: Sage.

West London Mental Health Trust (2009) *Independent Inquiry into the Care and Treatment of Peter Bryan and Richard Loudwell*. London: NHS London. Available at www.london.nhs.uk/publications/independent-publications/independent-inquiries/independent-reports-published-into-care-and-treatment-of-pb, accessed on 23 August 2011.

Wolfensberger, W. (1972) *The Principle of Normalization in Human Services*. Toronto: National Institute on Mental Retardation.

Wolfensberger, W. (1983) 'Social role valorization: A proposed new term for the principle of normalization.' *Mental Retardation 21*, 6, 234–239.

World Health Organization (WHO) (1992) *The International Statistical Classification of Diseases and Related Health Problems, Tenth Revision (ICD-10)*. Geneva: WHO.

Yelloly, M. and Henkel, M. (eds) (1995) *Learning and Teaching in Social Work: Towards Reflective Practice*. London: Jessica Kingsley Publishers.

Subject Index

Author Index